Fans of "RE:"

"Re: explains how to re:charge your life and your business. Re:ad it, implement it, and let's get out of this re:cession and start kicking butt again."

—**Guy Kawasaki,** Author of *Enchantment: The Art of Changing Hearts, Minds, and Actions*

"It's rare to find such honest advice in such an accessible format. This book will surely be a classic."

—**Jay Conrad Levinson**,
The Father of Guerrilla Marketing.
Author of, *"Guerrilla Marketing"* series of books

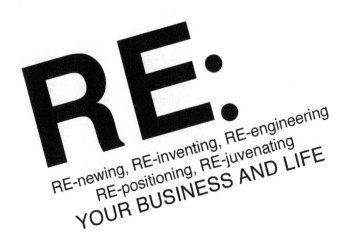

RE:

RE-newing, RE-inventing, RE-engineering
RE-positioning, RE-juvenating
YOUR BUSINESS AND LIFE

AL LAUTENSLAGER

NEW YORK

RE:

RE-newing, RE-inventing, RE-engineering, RE-positioning, RE-juvenating your Business and Life

by Al Lautenslager
© 2011 Al Lautenslager. All rights reserved.

ISBN 978-1-60037-992-5 Paperback
ISBN 978-1-60037-993-2 ePub Version
Library of Congress Control Number: 2011925304

Published by:

Morgan James Publishing
The Entrepreneurial Publisher
5 Penn Plaza, 23rd Floor
New York City, New York 10001
(212) 655-5470 Office
(516) 908-4496 Fax
www.MorganJamesPublishing.com

Cover Design by:
Rachel Lopez
rachel@r2cdesign.com

Interior Design by:
Bonnie Bushman
bbushman@bresnan.net

Acknowledgements

Acknowledgements are an author's opportunity to, not only thank those close, but also to reflect.

When I look back on my life there have been many instances of reinvention, repositioning, and reengineering. These usually had positive outcomes. These instances took my life in new directions, new positive directions. When I think of these situations there are usually key people in my life that were part of these changes. Those are the people I want to thank.

I could open up the flood gates of Re words when it comes to my wife Julie. She is my soul mate, my best friend, and my number one supporter. She believes in me in a way that gives me the inspiration to do all that I do. For that I am forever grateful. Julie, I love you.

I think back about the many redirection discussions I had with my parents. While they are both gone now in body, their spirit continues to drive me each and every day. Each of my own personal Re stories can somehow be connected to them or a lesson they taught me along the path of life.

My daughter, Allison, offers me perspectives that change me, reengineer some of my philosophy, and renew my thinking in many ways. While that may sound humorous, it is very serious and for that I hold her very close to my heart.

The rest of my family, sister Karen and her husband Dale, sister Pam and her husband Joe, and brother Steve showed me renewed levels of support when I most needed it and for that I thank them all.

Courtney and Bradley and now Chaz, Caden and Carsen Brown entered my life in new ways and repositioned my thinking even more.

Extended family of Max, Di, Marc and Steve bring me renewed feelings of what family means. Thank you.

The countless friends, too numerous to mention, (you know who you are) offer renewed and ongoing ties for life. Thanks to all of you.

From the professional side of this project I am indebted to David Hancock, Founder of Morgan James Publishing. I led him and now he has led me to the culmination of this book. Thank you David, and thanks to all others at Morgan James Publishing. Thank you also to my main editor, Dianne Morr, a true example of how a thriving network can come back into play renewed after many years.

There are others to thank, I'm sure. For those not mentioned, thank you. I look forward to continuing to change minds and to influence in future books.

And then there's Lu.

Contents

Acknowledgements iii

Preface vii

Introduction...1

CHAPTER 1: Renewal, Reinvention and Refreshing
In Action 7

CHAPTER 2: Renewal 19

CHAPTER 3: Reinvention 33

CHAPTER 4: Revitalization...49

CHAPTER 5: Repositioning 65

CHAPTER 6: Rejuvenation 75

CHAPTER 7: Reengineering...85

CHAPTER 8: Rethink and Rejoice:
Pursuing Personal Happiness....................95

CHAPTER 9: Reconsidering the Status Quo 107

Preface

As consumers wrestle with tightening credit, inflation, economic slowdown, unemployment, debt, the housing crises, global unrest, and prognostications of doom and gloom; doing something different is more important than ever.

To quote Mark Twain: "If you do what you've always done, you'll get what you always got." Repositioning, reengineering, renewing, reinventing, rejuvenating, and reenergizing are all becoming essential to close up space improving businesses, careers, hopes, dreams, personal development, and life in general. And yes, that includes your life.

This book is a message of hope and inspiration. This book teaches you how to understand life lessons through key principles that reposition your life for success and happiness. This book is recommended for anyone whose life has become stagnant and who wants to get out of that state, for those who want to move from mediocrity to excellence; for those who want to break out of status quo. It will help you to look at every area of your life and challenge you to move to the level you want to reach.

RE: is a great tool for examining your life, setting goals, living your vision, or recharging for that needed push. It is a book for people in a challenging state of life. It is my intention to provide you with a manual that is insightful, encouraging, engaging, motivational, and inspiring. *Re: The Book* is clearly a book for you if you want to make a change for the better.

RE: is for anyone ready to make necessary changes to be truly happy.

If you're not standing still in life, chances are one or all of these ideas are on your mind:

- Improving life
- Battling status quo
- Demonstrating ambition
- Pursuing happiness
- Dealing with change
- Exploring possibilities

All of these ideas are related to change, improvement, doing things again or differently, or re-_____ (insert your Re word of choice here). That is what this book is about.

The most important aspect of change is to move toward it. Make a decision and act; don't just wish and hope. Wishing and hoping are not strategies of action. *RE:* will motivate you to take the necessary action, make the necessary decisions, and take the necessary control of your life so that you can live the life you want.

The loud message before you here is to understand the perspective and apply the full meaning of Re words.

I understand the problems and challenges you face and offer ways to resolve them. I offer tools, tips, and techniques to further your knowledge, skills, and resources for growth, add development, and improvement. Many readers buy books to solve problems, fulfill a need, or to learn something they don't know. Using the Re concept, the information in this book is presented as knowledge restructured into bite-sized solutions for you.

This is an age of "new insecurity" in American life, says Micki McGee, author of *Self Help, Inc. Makeover Culture in American Life*. With divorce more prevalent and competition for jobs stiffer than ever, Americans can't just maintain their appearance or their job skills. They must constantly improve them. "We live in a society where we see ourselves as competitors, for jobs and affections," McGee says.

The good news is that you are not alone. This book is written for you and the many people in similar situations. Everybody can use renewal; everyone can rejuvenate, reinvent, or reengineer. Re is essential to the life of everyone who is not satisfied with where they are, not happy with their own status quo, or who feel stuck with their own inner feelings.

The benefits provided by this book include:

- Friendship (renewal)
- Emotional support (restructuring)
- Experimental knowledge (rejuvenation)
- Identity (reengineering)
- A sense of community and more

Coincidentally these are the exact benefits that the American Psychological Association *Dictionary of Psychology* says a book like this one provides.

Daniel Gilbert, a professor of psychology and Director of the Hedonic Psychology Laboratory at Harvard University, states that our own perceptions of happiness will change at different times of our lives.

It is because of this changing perception of happiness that people and organizations need to change as their quest takes different forms. This dynamic quest leads people and organizations to reposition, reengineer, rejuvenate, reinvent, renew, and revive, their mindset. There are many Re words that apply as people strive for happiness, success, or even just survival. For this book we will concentrate on the significant few.

People are always looking for ways to enrich their lives and improve their skills. Businesses and organizations are always looking for ways to grow and to contribute more. Sometimes for business, this is survival. Sometimes it is providing shareholder value and growth, jobs for employees, or social contributions for a better world. For people it is a never-ending quest for happiness.

Dan Baker, author of *What Happy People Know*, states his belief that the quest to achieve happiness will characterize the psychology of the 21st century. This kind of endeavor can change a whole culture and certainly can change lives.

The goal of this book is to change minds, to change thinking, and to offer perspectives so that individuals can change their lives and organizations can change for the better as well.

One inspiration for this book came from "The Paradox of History" by Dr. Bob Moorehead former pastor of Seattle's Overlake Christian Church. This essay has been widely circulated on the internet and has opened eyes and, hopefully, minds a little wider.

"The paradox of our time in history is that we have taller buildings, but shorter tempers; wider freeways, but narrower viewpoints. We spend more, but have less;

we buy more but enjoy it less. We have bigger houses and smaller families; more conveniences, but less time; we have more degrees, but less sense; more knowledge, but less judgment; more experts, but more problems; more medicine, but less wellness.

We drink too much, smoke too much, spend too recklessly, laugh too little, drive too fast, get too angry too quickly, stay up too late, get up too tired, read too seldom, watch TV too much, and pray too seldom.

We have multiplied our possessions, but reduced our values. We talk too much, love too seldom, and hate too often. We've learned how to make a living, but not a life; we've added years to life, not life to years.

We've been all the way to the moon and back, but have trouble crossing the street to meet the new neighbor. We've conquered outer space, but not inner space; we've done larger things, but not better things.

We've cleaned up the air, but polluted the soul; we've split the atom, but not our prejudice.

We write more, but learn less; we plan more, but accomplish less. We've learned to rush, but not to wait; we have higher incomes, but lower morals; we have more food, but less appeasement; we build more computers to hold more information to produce more copies than ever, but have less communication; we've become long on quantity, but short on quality.

These are the times of fast foods and slow digestion; tall men, and short character; steep profits, and shallow relationships. These are the times of world peace, but domestic warfare; more leisure, but less fun; more kinds of food, but less nutrition.

RE:

These are days of two incomes, but more divorce; of fancier houses, but broken homes. These are days of quick trips, disposable diapers, throw away morality, one-night stands, overweight bodies, and pills that do everything from cheer to quiet to kill.

It is a time when there is much in the show window and nothing in the stockroom; a time when technology has brought this letter to you, and a time when you can choose either to make a difference, or to just hit delete...

Introduction

Momentum for Re words has been building for several years. Bill Marvin, known as the Restaurant Doctor and Phyllis Ann Marshall, owner of Food Power, a highly respected restaurant consulting firm in Southern California, presented a Super Summit in 2007, and called it a 100,000 mile Tune- Up for Restaurants (www.supersummit.net). They described their event with many Re words to emphasize the need for constant improvement:

They sum it up by stating: "It looks like we can actually summarize the idea behind Super Summit in a few words: Re-Invent, Re-Vitalize, Re-Fresh, Re-Energize, Re-Position, Re-New, Re-Establish, Re-Orient, Re-Discover, Re-Invigorate... and Re-Tire! Now that will make one awesome 100,000 Mile Tune-Up!"

On January 20, 2009, Barack Obama clearly emphasized renewal in his inaugural address. As his first official act as our newly sworn-in president, he proclaimed a national day of renewal and reconciliation. "The story of America is one of renewal in the face of adversity, reconciliation in a time of discord," President Obama stated, describing the moment in time. Obama's statement of renewal was also reflected in his reference to "...a better history." While every new president brings change; change has been Obama's hallmark. His oratory called for mass change, the epitome of renewal. His statement of renewal for this very important time suggested we remake America.

Previous generations have seen dramatic changes throughout their lives with mechanical, technological, and scientific advances. While we will certainly see more brand new developments, we are now seeing many concepts rethought, redone, and revised. Now renewal is the primary strategy to be "better than before." In some businesses renewal is the only choice for improvement and, sometimes, for survival.

We see makeovers everywhere. People, companies, hairstyles, homes, financial situations, businesses are all undergoing makeovers. *RE Plastic Surgery*, a plastic and cosmetic surgery practice based in the West Midlands and Central England, United Kingdom, has named their practice RE. They are the epitome of improvement and change. This aptly named practice offers a comprehensive aesthetic and cosmetic plastic surgery service. They even explain the derivation of Re on their website: Re is a Latin prefix found in many English words. Its root meaning is back or again.

Using advanced plastic surgery techniques, their goals are to:

- Rebuild
- Rejuvenate
- Revitalize
- Reinvigorate
- Renew
- Restore
- Repair

While we are seeing tremendous attention to makeovers, the importance of revising and redoing is not a new idea. In the New York Times July 3, 1958 edition, Alfred Edward Palmer said, "After you've done things the same way for two years, look them over carefully. After five years look at them with suspicion and after 10 years throw them away and start all over." The same is even truer in today's world. Application of this definition clearly leads to a desire to refresh, remake, redo and renew in life, in business, personally, and professionally.

Frank Luntz, author of *Words That Work*, states that the Re words are incredibly powerful because they take the best elements or ideas from the past and apply them to the present and the future. He goes on to say, "…take the old and make it new again by putting a fresh spin on it with one or multiple Re words." Luntz singles out words like renew, revitalize, rejuvenate, restore, and rekindle as word vehicles related to taking something that is old, tired, or stale and giving it new passion and polish. To renew is to take an important product or corporate commitment and reassert it. To revitalize is to take something that is deteriorating and inject new life into it. To rejuvenate is to take something old and bring it up to date with a more youthful feel. To restore is to take something old and return it to its original luster. To rekindle is to inject emotion or passion into something tired and staid."

"The Re words imply action, movement, progress, and improvement—all the essential attributes in the twenty-first-century economy," according to Luntz. "Of course, Re words are perfect for a society obsessed with constant reinvention and makeover. The Re words speak to our sustained adolescence as many of us, despite being well into mid-life, still stubbornly refuse to accept the realization that life as it is now is, in fact, all there is."

Re is a useful prefix in English, typically signaling "again." Webster's New World College Dictionary, Fourth Edition goes on for pages and pages with Re verbs whose meanings are so self-explanatory that more Re words are simply listed in the bottom margin.

I agree with Luntz that Re words will have real staying power as we go through even more changes in the next decade whether related to communicating ideas, building integrity or informing audiences, customers, associates, friends, and family.

Anything related to a Re word is really a response to a change. Johann Wolfgang Van Goethe, a German dramatist, novelist, poet and scientist (1749-1832) is quoted as saying, "We must always change, renew, and rejuvenate ourselves: otherwise we harden."

Van Goethe also said, "To truly live is to be passionate about life and the possibilities it affords us. In today's world we all too often run across people who are just passing time; waiting for the 'good life' to simply come along." He goes on to state, "We do not need to tell you how fast paced our days have become. You need to breathe life back into your spirit so that you feel rejuvenated and alive again. Feel freedom from the things that interrupt your ability to truly live your life."

Life is full of changes and surprises. How will you respond to what life throws at you? Will you be prepared for those surprises? Chances are whatever your response, a Re word will be part of it, especially if what life throws at you is a curveball and something that doesn't contribute to the life you want to live.

Life is a process, a path and many have referred to it as a journey. We often hear "It's not the destination; it's the journey." Most of us, because of human nature, psychological, or environmental influences, want to make that journey the best one possible. If it is not what we want now, we must change and improve it. Change and improve are two words that resonate with all the Re words. Winston Churchill said, "To improve is to change."

Yes, there will be hurdles. Yes, there will be obstacles and yes, there will be curveballs. There will even be elation. Whatever is thrown at you has to be dealt with, for that is the key to making your life the journey that you want it to be.

Re words are all around us. It's time to gain the proper perspective on how our lives can change for the better. It's time to adapt and understand that the Re words are the key to making that happen.

Renewal, Reinvention and Refreshing In Action

DOING SOMETHING NEW FOR A NEW GENERATION IN NEW TIMES FOR NEW RESULTS

Life as we know it today needs to be renewed, revisited, reinvented, and revived. Supporters of the theory of Creationism believe that the Earth is 6,000 years old; others put it at 4.56 billion years old. In order to sustain, thrive, or even exist, continuous renewal must take place. Pepsi® modeled this when it came up with the Pepsi Refresh Project in 2009. The Pepsi Refresh Project is a multi-million dollar marketing platform that invites people to submit and vote for ideas that help make the world a better place. This is renewal in action and at its finest.

The Pepsi Refresh Project is a first-of-its-kind experiment in "reinventing" marketing. At the introduction of the project and campaign in 2010, Pepsi shifted one-third of its marketing budget to interactive and social media marketing. In what was considered a bold move, Pepsi pulled its high-profile, high-dollar

Super Bowl television commercials in favor of a digitally focused social-responsibility campaign. Consumers didn›t seem to mind. In the weeks leading up to the Super Bowl in 2010, Pepsi was the second most discussed advertiser associated with the Super Bowl, according to Nielsen. At the time, Pepsi's Refresh Project and overall social project was considered one of the most incredible initiatives undertaken by a major consumer brand.

As part of Pepsi's project, which at the time of this writing is still underway, consumers apply for grants ranging from $5,000 to $250,000 in one of six areas: health, arts and culture, food and shelter, the planet, neighborhoods, and education. Consumers vote on the winning projects. Pepsi awarded $14,545,000 as of December 2010.

In addition, Pepsi had the hope that the Refresh campaign would renew relationships with its consumers. Even though the brand has a youthful target and appeal, Pepsi is still positioned and thought of by many as the drink of multiple generations. Sustainability, that is, using resources in a way that does not deplete them, is a high priority to all generations. In thinking about making a difference and solving the great problems of our times, the concept of sustainability comes to the forefront. Whether it is your generation now, past generations, or the generations of the future, all need to be thinking for the long-term. Pepsi executives thought about this and hoped that their Pepsi's Refresh Project would keep the concept of sustainability top-of-mind along with the necessary degree of renewal, rejuvenation, and reinvention.

Cheryl Damian, a director in the cause-branding group at Cone, Inc. (a strategy and communications agency engaged in building brand trust) observed that "this is big, new, getting a lot of attention. It›s impactful; it›s innovative."

The launching of the Refresh campaign was Pepsi's attempt to celebrate optimism, a key component to any renewal. They also wanted to celebrate and proclaim their role in a changing world; a changing world built on renewal, reinvention, and rejuvenation. Pepsi clearly wanted the brand to be an optimistic catalyst for idea creation leading to an "ever-refreshing" world.

Just as a side note, part of the launch of the newer, fresh campaign was a result of Pepsi's strategically deciding to partner with a new advertising and marketing agency. When that announcement came forward, Dave Burwick, the chief marketing officer for the PepsiCo North America beverages division, stated that the change in agencies is being made to "refresh" Pepsi's communications. His comment was a hidden clue in what was about to come—the Pepsi Refresh campaign and project. Burwick went on to say that the initiative was intended "to reinvigorate Pepsi's legacy of leading-edge advertising and marketing." Pepsi's campaign was driven by the underlying "Re" concepts refresh, renew, and reinvigorate.

The Pepsi Refresh campaign was preceded by an effort to reinvent their brand. Media communication and marketing messaging at the time of the brand reinvention and the project introduction read:

PEPSICO KICKS-OFF BRAND REINVENTION CAMPAIGN WITH NEW PACKAGING / NEW TV SPOTS DURING SUPER BOWL

"Refresh Everything" Press Conference Unveils PepsiCo's Brand Strategy to Breathe New Energy into the Beverage Sector

Wednesday, January 28, 2009, New York, NY: At a press conference in New York City this week, PepsiCo North America Beverages® formally unveiled a portfolio-wide reinvention strategy with new advertisements, new packaging, and new TV and Super Bowl spots designed to breathe new energy into the beverage sector.

PepsiCo's marquee beverage brands include Pepsi, Tropicana, SoBe Lifewater, and Gatorade. The nation's largest TV audience will witness dramatic changes in some of America's most revered beverage brands.

The highlights of PepsiCo's select brand-by-brand reinvention will include: Pepsi Building on a 100-year legacy, the new logo and Pepsi Refresh campaign taps into a wave of re-energization and optimism that is sweeping across America.

The latest campaign again embodies the spirit of youth while building a bridge between yesterday and today. In the upcoming "Refresh Anthem" spot, Grammy award-winning artist Will.i.am performs legendary Bob Dylan's "Forever Young" to a visual collage of iconic images celebrating generations past and present. An apt way to bring Pepsi's "Every Generation Refreshes the World" brand belief to life.

The Pepsi Refresh Project grantees are estimated to have reached over 200,000 people across the country at the time of this writing, with over 7,500 ideas submitted and over 250 grants awarded, not to mention that millions and millions of consumers cast votes in this social marketing project. A wide variety of ideas have been funded through the project, everything from building playgrounds in communities across the U.S., to providing instruments to students, and supporting energy efficiency installations. Pepsi will continue to help move communities forward in renewal and reinvention by supporting local ideas through this groundbreaking program, observers proclaim. Based on its success and impact, Pepsi will continue to fund the Pepsi Refresh Project and intends to launch the program in Europe, Latin America, and Asia in 2011.

Renewal, reinvention, rejuvenation, and reengineering does not have to happen on a grand scale all the time. The Pepsi Refresh Project has demonstrated that bringing simple ideas to life can create a powerful impact in local communities. Here are just a few examples of the projects dedicated to renewal and reinvention leading to Pepsi's goal of an ever-refreshing world:

- Let our US troops know Americans care for them, by sending care packages.

- Fund research and find a cure for the metabolic disorder PKU.

- Teach youth the power of video media.

- Replace Rusted Animal Kennels, Equipment and Beds: Project-Community Animal Rescue & Adoption, Inc. (CARA, Inc.)

- Help us build their field of dreams-Miracle League of Lawton-Fort Sill.

- Produce SMART BINZ Solar Powered Recycling Receptacles.

- Help at-risk youth use art to address social issues and build community.

- Save The Gateway Playhouse Theater Collaborative of South Jersey.

- Construct a handicapped accessible playground for all students - McHenry Primary PTO Rome, Georgia.

- Give Beads of Courage to children with serious illnesses.

Pepsi's renewed approach to marketing is a lesson in the reinvention of marketing and business. The new approach was based on Pepsi's long-standing belief in the power of people and their ideas to make positive change. It was facilitated by the growth of social media platforms that enabled them to have ongoing conversations with customers, explore the whole notion of two-way communication, and to explore new ways of driving social engagement and interaction.

Pepsi explains this renewed approach pretty simply: With the tools of the social web, the interaction between brands and their consumers is now a two-way street. This engagement leads to a meaningful dialogue; and in the instance of the Pepsi Refresh Project, it leads to meaningful changes in communities across the U.S.

Something New for a New Generation in New Times Brings New Results

Pepsi is not the only major consumer brand company to have a Refresh campaign and not the only organization to think renewal. KFC®, previously known as Kentucky Fried Chicken®, has started to launch a number of unique, non-traditional marketing campaigns all focused on changing the consumer's current brand perceptions. These smaller campaigns are happening during the same timeframe as KFC's announcement to renovate and renew 50 stores nationwide. According to KFC, the first renewed and refreshed store will open up in the company's hometown of Louisville, KY, and it will look, smell, and feel different to consumers.

KFC also launched its Refresh Pothole Program beginning in its home city of Louisville, KY. The company offered to fill potholes in exchange for stamping their logo on the refreshed pothole. KFC even dressed individuals in the Colonel's iconic outfit and sent them out to fix the city's dilapidated roads. Once a pothole was filled in, the company would label the pothole with the words "Refreshed by KFC" in a non-permanent, white, street chalk stencil. KFC chose the word refreshed in order to remind consumers that the chain uses only fresh chicken that is shipped weekly to its stores. The company has offered the service to a number of strategically selected U.S. cities. Here is their letter of invitation announcing their renewal effort:

Dear Mayor:

It is estimated that U.S. roads are riddled with more than 350 million potholes nationwide—that's one for every man, woman and child in America! Because of long, harsh winters and heavy traffic, cities everywhere are left with more potholes than ever. Add in the fact that asphalt is an expensive product, and the cost of those repairs is higher than ever.

Because of the financially tough times, many cities are delaying construction projects because they need to spend money patching these potholes instead. Some cities are even being forced to cut back on road services and maintenance crews. We at KFC understand that filling every one of these potholes is important and we're here to help!

In honor of our "Fresh Tastes Best"® campaign, we want to come and Re-"Fresh" your roads! The Colonel and his crew are on a mission to help out America and sponsor your city's "Fresh"ly repaired roads. Every patched pothole comes with the Colonel's very own stamp of approval.

KFC has been bringing communities together over buckets of chicken for more than 50 years. We invite you and your city to become a part of a new tradition and accept our offer to Re-"Fresh" your roads. Together, we can give your community a much-needed break and help keep America moving.

Sincerely,
Roger Eaton, President of KFC

Some individuals think that it's great that someone is taking care of the potholes, while others think it's just another coy marketing scheme. No matter what, KFC's renewal and rebranding efforts, in addition to its market rejuvenation, have people talking about their brand. KFC extends their Re thinking by calling the campaign, an "infrastructure renewal program."

In both cases, KFC's renewed marketing efforts and Pepsi's Refresh campaign are clear examples of doing something new for a new generation in new times that has produced new results!

Making Things Better

In 2010, Jeffrey Immelt, chairman and CEO of the General Electric Corp.® discussed the state of the economy, his company, America, and the future. In his discussion, Immelt stated that: "We have recently suffered one of the worst global economic downturns in history. The banking system teetered on the abyss. The financial sector suffered losses that will exceed $3 trillion. Unemployment surpassed 10 percent in the United States and rose even higher in many parts of the world. Asset prices across key segments plummeted. People lost faith in the principles of free markets and their power to create wealth and opportunities."

He went on to state that, "The world has been reset. Today's uncertainty feels like the 'new normal.' We will not return to the relative tranquility of the pre-crisis world. Growth will be harder to come by, trends will be more volatile, and constituent voices will be louder. We see this environment as an opportunity to renew GE."

Immelt was quick to realize that we are in a new generation, that evolution of business and economies does require change and in order to prosper, survive, thrive, and continue in the new market environment; renewal, reinvention, repositioning, reengineering, and more must be at the forefront of that evolution. Immelt stated in GE's 2009 annual report that "Managing size and complexity was a strength for GE during a generation of economic stability. The world we live in today has more systemic risk. So GE must change." This was written in an annual report sprinkled with all of the Re words you are becoming familiar with here. The front cover of the report has the GE logo and eight words along with its title. Those words were used to define Immelt's message, GE's vision and strategies, as well as their overall feeling about the future. The words were: Reset, Re-imagine, Reinvest, Rethink, Research, Relationships, Responsibility and Renew. From Reset to Renew Immelt communicated the company's renewal message.

Here are the highlights of his renewal message that pertain to big business but can be applied to any company and organization:

- GE must be an industrial company first.
- GE must simplify and focus around core competitive advantages.
- GE must have a tighter focus on operations and liquidity.
- GE must have stronger processes around enterprise risk management and capital allocation.

- GE's goal is to have improved productivity and lower overhead cost.

- GE needs a more conservative cash profile to better prepare for volatility.

- GE will be repositioned as a simplified portfolio focused on infrastructure.

- GE is dedicated to investing in profitable growth.

- GE wants to create market solutions to tough societal problems.

- GE will have an energized and accountable team.

- GE will be a tough-minded and optimistic growth company.

After his review of these core principles and renewal guidelines, Immelt stated that GE wants to help lead an American growth renewal backed by GE's increased investment in more technology than at any other time in the company's history. As a result, GE is rebuilding manufacturing capability. It is selling products in every corner of the world. It is one of the country's biggest exporters, with $18 billion in export-related revenue. They are financing small and medium-sized companies and working with them to grow their businesses. Immelt said, "We want to be a company that is always getting better; a company that understands where it fits in markets and in society—and appreciates its responsibility to both. A company that makes better the great nation that made possible its success." The key renewal principle stated and practiced here is, "…that is always getting better." Reinvention makes them better. Renewal improves. Positive change is good. Jeffrey Immelt knows this. GE practices this. Renewal will happen. GE will always get better.

Jeffrey Immelt is proud to share that his company is beginning a "renewal" that should be financially attractive to investors, while positioning GE to lead, and shareowners to prosper, as new systems and values for the global economy are created. This is a major commitment to renewal. Leadership and prosperity are two outcomes of renewal.

General Electric touts its commitment to renewal beyond just their annual report and their Chairman's message. In July of 2010, G.E. released their Annual Citizenship Report entitled, *Renewing Responsibilities*. The report covered GE's worldwide operations for the 2009 fiscal year and was structured around the discussion of three pillars of GE's strategy - energy and climate change, sustainable healthcare, and community building. The report also included an in-depth discussion of the relationship between business and society: how GE's people, products, and services help to enable prosperous and productive communities around the world. Among the financial forecast, philosophy, and vision statements, the report highlighted GE's commitment to renewal: "Based on our commitments to integrity, performance, and learning, GE is renewing our company coming out of this economic reset."

Renewal can be a central theme guiding a multi-billion dollar corporation, a small business, a professional practice, or an organization. It can also be a theme that guides you through life and its challenges. In a speech for the Detroit Economic Club at a June, 2010, Technology Center opening, Immelt continued his renewal message on a broader, more personal level. Entitled *An American Renewal*, the speech focused on the need for U.S. businesses to aggressively invest in research and development and export-driven manufacturing if the country is to successfully emerge from a "reset" economy. He said "…

change can come, but it requires a new way of thinking. It requires a clear and determined plan of action. It requires a stiff dose of candor about the troubles we face, many of which we brought on ourselves. It requires leaders throughout the economy to take command of events."

The world has been reset. Now we must lead an aggressive American renewal to win in the future. We should create an American industrial renewal by moving on five fronts:

- Invest in new technology.
- Win where it counts in clean energy and affordable health care.
- Become a country that is good at manufacturing and exports.
- Embrace public-private partnerships.
- Promote leaders who are also good citizens.

It is time to think big again. We must hold ourselves to a higher standard and we must renew America's economy to embrace the same kind of dream that transformed this country and this world not so long ago.

General Electric's commitment to renew itself, along with Pepsi's and KFC's decisions to reinvent and refresh themselves; are just a few of the new directions many companies take today. Without these renewed directions, companies grow stagnant, decline, or die. Without the commitment to renewal, things don't get better. GE, Pepsi, and KFC are making things better. So can you.

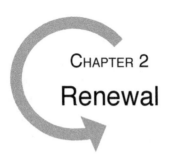

CHAPTER 2

Renewal

The word renew has often been used when "exploring the new" is involved. That is certainly the context of any urban renewal project. Johann Wolfgang Goethe used the word renew in his famous quotation about change: "We must always change, renew, rejuvenate ourselves; otherwise we harden." The concept of renewal involves the infusion of energy, renewed vitality, a new sense of purpose, or new sense of commitment. Renewal involves the examination of values, aspirations, sense of self, commitment, and connection to larger purposes.

In Stanley Gryskiewisz's book, *Positive Turbulence: Developing Climates for Creativity, Innovation and Renewal,* not only does he use the word renewal in the title but he states later in the book: "In a time of rapid and relentless change, the healthiest organizations continually renew themselves to thrive in a challenging environment." Just as urban renewal explores, investigates, and pursues the new; so do corporations and businesses. Corporate or business renewal is mostly associated with bringing the corporation or business "back to life."

A generation ago, we didn't hear much about business renewal. Why? Businesses weren't failing. When Penn Central Railroad failed in the early '70's, American industry was shocked and surprised. How could a pillar of the Industrial Revolution and the American economy fail? For the first time, American business got a surprising wake-up call.

Today, business bankruptcies are at an all time high. The "business of renewal" is correspondingly at a new level. Add to that controversial corporate scandals, compromised business ethics, excessive executive compensation, and other corporate/business and cultural violations at high levels, the result is all companies face challenging times—times that could potentially suck the life right out of them. In times like these, companies need to be revived, to be restored by an aggressive period of renewal to return their former vitality.

Even businesses that are currently thriving and achieving levels of success need to be aware of the need for renewal. T.D. Jakes, the ministerial and business visionary, entrepreneurial trailblazer, and spiritual shepherd to millions around the globe, warns that care must be taken to avoid complacency and arrogance— a sure ticket to the need for renewal.

In many of these cases, renewal is necessary not only for change but also for survival. Whether it's a business or a person, what is really at hand here is change, the willingness to change, and the desire to change for the better. John W. Gardner, author of *Self Renewal*, states that the factors that produce deterioration in people and societies are caused mostly by the failure to deal with change.

Businesses are usually thinking "renewal." Just like people, they want things better, they want happiness within their businesses, and they want smooth sailing. Business renewal is not just reserved for major corporations either. Small businesses, independent professionals, and family shops all participate in renewal or have a renewal attitude.

The lifeblood of business growth, longevity, value creation, and even survival is in finding new business opportunities, developing new relationships, and implementing new processes. These are also the underlying principles of renewal.

This type of renewal takes strategic evaluation and direction, innovation, business and client development, business marketing, employee development, and streamlined business management principles. That's exactly what happened with Konz Wood Products, a family-owned sawmill-turned-pallet manufacturer in Black Creek, Wisconsin. A Wisconsin business journal reported that Konz Wood Products, like their raw materials of trees, has proven renewable with perseverance and adaptability, both the seedlings of growth.

Their president, one of the brothers who own the company, has realized that there has to be a degree of flexibility to meet changing marketing demands as well as environmental influences. He says that every generation of their family has produced something different within their business. Some things have stayed the same: core values, business philosophies, family virtues, and the basic root of their products. On the other hand markets, demands, processes, and the world around business all changes. Response to these changes requires renewal. Konz Wood Products' renewal is based on perseverance, flexibility, and adaptability, primarily in their ever-evolving product and service offering.

The family was recognized for their efforts when Konz Wood Products earned the aptly named Second Wind Award as part of the Wisconsin Family Business Awards program, for their willingness through the decades to change its approach and to renew as market demanded.

Once again the underlying principle of change is present in this renewal. For the Konz family business, this evolution started with land clearing services. Next came the creation of a sawmill to produce and sell lumber to people to build homes on the cleared land. The next generation saw an opportunity in the manufacturing of wooden-veneer cheese boxes. This opportunity waned as competitive packaging took hold. The next Konz family member in line pursued a deal with Kimberly-Clark Corp. to produce crating for cellulose insulation shipping. This brought in other paper companies to work with Konz. Each step of the way, this family-owned business was experiencing their own renewal venturing into the production of wooden fences. After that business arm was sold off, the Konz's then concentrated on the business that has fueled their growth to their current concentration on their wooden pallet business.

While modern manufacturing and processing techniques were critical in their renewal, a new approach to the Konz family business ownership was just as critical. Only family members that participate in the business now enjoy ownership. With ownership comes profits and the new outlook of the participating family members is to plow the profits back into the business, renewing with fresh resources. Evolution requires renewal. Longevity requires renewal. Success requires renewal. Konz Wood Products understands renewal and has evolved for generations in creative and successful ways.

Rejuvenation, renewal, and revitalization are really pursuing the life you desire. Hotel Valley Ho in Scottsdale, AZ offers a spa retreat dedicated to "Inner Urban Renewal." This retreat is advertized as a revitalizing.two-day retreat focused on decompression, detoxification, and delight. The private sessions of the retreat are designed to transform the client's way of living on a physical, mental, and emotional level, creating lasting changes so one can live the life one desires.

Sometimes renewal happens by doing nothing. Yes, I meant that literally. Look how busy everyone is these days: jam packed schedules, unreasonable deadlines, too many appointments, people to meet, kids to shuttle, and the list goes on. Stress is at high levels because of any one or all of these. Imagine eliminating one or all of these constraints. Imagine no cell phones ringing or emails bombarding you. Yes, you are probably thinking, "What a dream world." Being in that dream world is a form of renewal. That is what a vacation is supposed to be: a break, a rest; time out from life that provides a refreshed feeling and a renewed spirit and definitely recharged batteries. These breaks are imperative for renewal to happen.

Companies, always striving for growth, build on becoming new again. Individuals adjust their life direction when becoming new again; renewal in the greatest sense.

I know you are probably now thinking that all of this is much easier said than done; much easier to write in a book then actually carry out. With a few steps, a few planned actions, a deliberate initiative, you can let go, recharge, and renew. The following components can be the basis of your renewal plan; your renewal road map. Each one of these could command its own book, article, or chapter but they are presented here as ideas to get your renewal mindset working.

Take a Step Back

In the world of warfare, taking a step back is known as a retreat. Under the same context, taking a step back might imply surrender, giving up, a calculated or non-calculated withdrawal, all with a negative connotation. However, the contrary is many times the case. "Zoning Out" and gaining perspective on the big picture can be positive.

Companies have retreats of all kinds for various purposes such as spiritual, teambuilding, innovation, and so on. Getting away from the daily routine, the hustle bustle of everyday life, and the media and taking time to reflect, think, and breathe, all breed a new beginning or a new direction; a renewal.

A step back can take the form of a vacation, trip, seclusion, or any downtime away from the routine. Let the mind and body both take that step back. Breaks, vacations, time-outs can produce renewed feelings of excitement, exuberance, and pleasure. Peace and fulfillment soon follow—true renewal.

A break from the routine and a break from the things you see, hear, and experience day in and day out allow you to consider new perspectives. Those new perspectives could solve your most vexing problems, meet your loftiest challenge, or present that one opportunity you have been seeking. As your mind is freed from the usual, day-to-day worries and responsibilities, fresh ideas pop into your mind. Renewal happens.

⤷ Don't Be One of the 80 Percent

Eighty percent of small business owners check email or voice mail while on vacation, according to a survey conducted by Thomas Industrial Network and The U.S. Small Business

Administration. Try not to be one of those 80 percent. Checking in to the office dilutes the whole power of renewal and the process itself.

True renewal allows us to let go of the stress we encounter in everyday life. True renewal recharges our batteries for living. This means that the renewal vacation is not only all about visiting a nice, sunny, warm paradise. It's a matter of mentally letting go, mentally recharging, and creating a renewed state of mind.

Continuous Learning

You can become a new person through continuous learning. The people who support a company or organization can make it a new one with continuous learning. In order to gain a positive contribution from continuous learning, there has to be an inherent desire to learn; a realization that learning will improve situations and be positive.

Fresh learning and new information allows for the handling of change and challenges. Labeling yourself as a lifelong learner is a tremendous mindset that lets the learning happen.

Go ahead. Say it. "I am a lifelong learner." Now go learn something new!

Just like a child would do, asking why questions and getting answers results in continuous learning. Fresh learning contributes to problem solving. Problem solving contributes to renewal.

⤷ Note: Some of these tips and techniques overlap. Continuous learning could consist of reading, seeking out a mentor or doing something different and new, away from the routine. These renewal components are covered in other chapters.

Innovation

Mark Victor Hansen, co-author with Jack Canfield of the Chicken Soup for the Soul series of books stated that there are two inherent business skills required for the 21st century: Innovation and Networking. This applies to business and life and both contribute to renewal.

Innovation, fed by creativity, sets businesses and organizations apart from each other and provides a competitive advantage. Innovation in life allows for dealing with new challenges, new environments, and new situations that often appear in unpredictable ways. Renewal allows for dealing with the "new" described here.

⤷ The Center for Corporate Renewal in Plainfield, New Jersey, (www.ctrforcorporaterenewal.com) helps business leaders overcome nagging problems with profitability, performance, innovation, and change by teaching them how to build a core capability for *corporate renewal*. *Corporate renewal* is based on a proven set of leadership and management tools that foster sustainable levels of performance excellence, marketplace adaptability, profitable growth, and continuous innovation.

The Center defines Corporate Renewal as the ability to:

- **Think with a strategic focus by making** sense of a changing environment and gaining focus on the next right strategic move.
- **Act with disciplined execution by aligning and mobilizing an** entire organization behind a new strategic focus.
- **Lead with creative renewal**: Renew the entrepreneurial spirit, while enabling your organization to continually cycle through stronger and stronger strategy-to-execution phases.

Innovation is an integral process of these activities.

Planning

"If you don't know where you're going, how will you know when you get there?" That's a question we hear often. How do you know which paths to take, which turns to make, and what speed to go? You know none of this without a plan. Without a plan, how do you know what needs to become new again? How do you know where renewal should happen?

Planning doesn't mean cranking out massive documentation. Planning simply means having a conscious awareness of what's next, what's needed, what's wanted, what's not wanted, what direction to take, and what the desired end point looks like. That's it. This is not a book on planning. It is a renewal book. Planning leads to renewal. That's it.

Note: Regardless of how well you plan, life does not proceed along a predetermined, black and white pathway. Being able to deal with life's curveballs, unexpected situations, surprises, and roadblocks requires flexibility and a contingency mindset.

Nimbleness, contingency planning, and flexibility go hand in hand with planning and all contribute to renewal.

Action and Implementation

Planning is one thing; taking action is another. Implementation is one of the top challenges of individuals, businesses, and organizations today. Once you have a plan, focus on just a few things to implement for renewal. Focus on what you can do completely and comfortably in a financial and emotional sense. Most people and businesses can't do everything planned. If you can, great! But in the spirit of renewal, there is no need to put undue pressure on yourself. Some is better than none. You have my permission not to do everything in your plan. Start small and work towards accomplishing more. Just implement. (I was going to say Just Do It! but that phrase was taken.)

Many books and articles have been written on getting things done. That sole subject is beyond the scope of this book. Understand implementation, apply the major points, and take action for renewal. That is definitely within the scope of this book.

Don't Strive for or Expect Perfection

I know the heading to this paragraph surprised some readers as being somewhat counterintuitive, but bear with me here.

Establishing expectations is part of planning and implementation. Establishing reasonable expectations is essential. Unreasonable expectations, the mantra of corporate brainwash of the '80s and '90s (I know. I was there) led to inefficiencies, burnout, tension, complacency, breakup, and demise, personally and professionally. Good enough might be good enough. I have transformed many businesses through my own form of brainwashing with the simple mantra "Done is better than perfect." Don't let the attainment of perfection be a distraction to your own renewal or your business or organization renewal. Many will want to high five me after reading this short, yet *significant* paragraph. I feel renewed by writing it and reading it again.

Dealing with the Unpleasant

Dealing with something unpleasant doesn't sound like something that will renew mind, body, and spirit; it can with the right mindset and attitude. There are things in life and business that you have to deal with even if you hate it. It's true for you and everyone else.

An entrepreneur has to deal with business support functions, even if she doesn't like it. People avoid confrontation of all types but sometimes it has to be dealt with. Think of income tax filing preparation. This is typically an unpleasant task but once done, the feeling of accomplishment takes over. Getting the large, unpleasant tasks done and behind you allow you to feel renewed, kind of like letting out a big "Whew!" when done. Whew! = renewal.

Seeking and Accepting Help

Asking questions of someone more experienced than you, of someone with more expertise, leads to renewal. A guru or mentor can offer information, act as a counselor or confidant, and advise accordingly. A mentor can expand your network and point you in directions that will be favorable to your renewal.

The larger and more overriding factor in seeking out an expert or mentor is admitting that you need one, that one can benefit you, and that you are willing to subscribe to the help or information received. Seek out a knowledgeable associate or advisor to help you and become renewed.

Physical Care, Physical Stimulation, Relaxation

Over time, our bodies and minds accumulate and adjust to the aches, pains, and physical bad habits that occur along life's journey. Becoming new again means doing things to overcome these aches and pains while teaching the body new habits. Typically, even with some initial hurt, doing these things feels good. Recovery from pain, fatigue, stress, or other negative physical influence contributes to a higher quality of daily life. Everyone is different. It is up to you to identify what feels good to you physically and implement the appropriate physical activity into your daily routine, leading to a renewed state of physical being.

Makeover/New Identity

We can all thank the popularity of reality television shows to bring the term and concept of "makeover" to the forefront of pop culture and all of our lives. On television, makeover is related to improvements such as makeup, hair styling, and physical appearance. This branched out to house remodeling and makeovers; to make new again, the ultimate in renewal in the form of a complete re-do.

The makeover concept will work for businesses as well as individuals. A business makeover might mean new processes, new products, new identity, a new logo or identity, and more. An individual makeover might mean a new hairstyle, a different color make-up, new identity/appearance, and more. Choose what you want to make new again, just like the makeover concept, and work towards the change; the change to become renewed.

Do Something Fun

Just as getting an unpleasant task out of the way can make you feel renewed, accomplishing pleasant tasks feels just as renewing. If you had it your way, you might only do fun things, pleasant tasks, things you like. Unfortunately doing this 100 percent of the time is not practical and not what life deals us. However, sometimes you don't proactively do enough of the pleasant. One form of renewal is doing things you like. Plan a fun activity, do something that brings you complete enjoyment and puts a smile on your face. And associate with people you like. Think it, plan it, and do it. Don't always let the unpleasant push aside the pleasant. You will definitely be renewed the more you smile, laugh, and have fun.

Stimulate the Senses

Life itself puts everyone in a state of flux, always working towards combating the stresses that occur with aging. These stresses affect our physical wellbeing along with every other sense. Stimulating the senses renews each and every one of us.

Stimulating the senses for personal renewal can take many forms: aromatherapy, massage, listening to music, reading, and more. Giving the body a time out renews the senses. You deserve to feel good. A little pampering puts you on "top of the world" or "on cloud nine" which are both renewed states of being.

Sleep/Rest/Nap/Do Nothing

"What? I have permission to do nothing? I don't always have to be active and productive? Wow, what a feeling." That is the feeling of true renewal.

Life has become faster-paced and more complex. Many people are always in a hurry. Everyone is running and running and running on the treadmill of life. Renewal can't happen if you stay on that treadmill continuously. The human body and mind are not genetically set up for unlimited exertion. That's why sleep was created. It is up to you to use this invention if you want to be renewed. Effectively we renew ourselves every night and with every nap, every break, and every rest. Once again, get it in your head that it's OK to take a nap. The world will keep spinning. Guaranteed. The sun will continue to rise and you will still be useful. Guaranteed. A renewed state is a productive state. Sleep is a renewing and necessary life process. Use it.

Scot Silverstein, M.D., states that basic training in the Marines is easier than a year of medical internship because basic training is much shorter and the marines have a regular schedule of sleep time during their training. A medical internship is a physical and mental marathon, complete with a range of emotional cycles 24 hours a day. A marine will feel more renewed after basic training than the medical professional.

These renewal strategies work. Pick the ones that work for you. Some of them might not be for you. You won't know until you implement them. Your goal is renewal. Renewal takes different forms and different shapes for different people. Figure out the best form and shape for you and you are guaranteed the ultimate feeling of renewal. Yes, renewal happens!

CHAPTER 3

Reinvention

Reinvention comes into play when things are dying or in deep decline, much like the classified advertising section of most of today's newspapers. Newspapers' weakness in classified ads is becoming fatal for many dailies. Revenues that support reporting, the primary purpose of newspapers, are plunging in deep declines.

There is much discussion, inside and outside the newspaper industry, regarding how daily newspaper operations can resurrect their sagging classified ad sector. The website, www. ReinventingClassifieds.com is a website devoted to that very issue. The tagline says it all: Traditional Classifieds Are Broken; Let's Work Together to Reinvent Them. It further states that **the_website is about bringing together industry voices to reinvent, reinvigorate, and SAVE newspaper classifieds. (The Re word beat goes on.)** On this site, ideas for reinvention are many and varied. Many suggest mirroring the online advertising business models:

- Offer inexpensive or free content placement.
- Categorize and sort information.
- Write content augmenting classified (Generate revenue from that which is being reported on.)

- Treat ads as content.

- Reconsider need to print classified ads daily.

Solicit ads that are local, relevant, and of real value to subscribers.

It still remains a question whether this formula is enough to reinvent classifieds even to the point of survival. Only time will tell. However, not attempting any kind of reinvention is a sure ticket to the newspaper graveyard.

Whether you are a business owner or manager, an organization member, or just you; chances are you have been or will be involved in some kind of transition. This transition could be personal or professional. Maybe you aspire to a new position, new job, new company, or even a new career. Businesses aspire to new profit and growth levels. Organizations always work toward reaching more people, creating more awareness, and gaining more contributors. The common thread here is all of these entities want to become something or someone they currently aren't. That takes reinvention.

The Reinvention Mindset

Reinvention requires a whole new mindset and approach to your new goal is. It may require more imagination, analysis, understanding, and culture. Or it may simply require more hard work and an attitude of relentless pursuit.

You can do the same thing. You can reinvent yourself, your team, your company or organization for success. Benjamin Franklin continually thought about reinvention as it related to himself and his personal life. He focused on one virtue a month each year—plus humility, which he worked on all year round on the advice of a detractor! He established 13 virtues that he deemed necessary to reinvent himself. He felt so strongly about these that he shared them with everyone who would listen and accept the notion that these virtues could apply to anyone. Franklin's goal, whether it was reinvention, rejuvenation, or a reengineering of his life was to master all of his stated virtues.

Franklin worked on his list relentlessly and eventually reached an epiphany. But it was a meaningful realization of a different kind. He discovered that mastery of 12 of the virtues contradicted the mastery of the 13th—humility. So, he planned his work on virtues as monthly goals and considered the attempt at mastery of humility a continual, ongoing effort; something to strive towards constantly with the mindset of reinvention, not perfection.

 Franklin's Virtues List

- Temperance
- Silence
- Order
- Resolution
- Frugality
- Industry
- Sincerity
- Justice
- Moderation
- Cleanliness
- Tranquility
- Chastity

Reinvention Best Practices and Best Attitudes

Beyond Franklin's self-motivated aspirations, many of life's changes related to reinvention involve career changes, job changes, or position changes. The best practices and best attitudes to make these changes are based on reinvention. Let's look at some related points:

- Emphasize quality of life more than the job. Living the life you love should be one of the end results of a job. Therefore, avoid any potential happiness conflicts.

- Release unrealistic ideas. Things won't be perfect each time you reinvent. That's why you should think about reinvention over and over, much like Benjamin Franklin did. Reinvention doesn't end after doing it once. If you think life will be perfect when you reach your reinvention goal, you will surely be in for one big surprise. You, too, will be adding Franklin's thirteenth virtue of humility to your list. Those who reinvent most successful do it over and over and over. Just ask Ben.

- Evolve, don't just act and stop. Reinvention can be considered a process. One path of reinvention may lead to another path that wasn't part of your initial reinvention plan or part of your dream. Think discovery; think rediscovery; think reinvention.

- Avoid complacency at all costs. In her book *Danger in the Comfort Zone*, author Judith Bardwick stresses the importance of getting outside your comfort zone as a way that forces a change fundamental to reinvention.

- You aren't who you used to be. If you're reinvented, you're someone new. Grab hold of this new identity and run with it. Run with it until your identity is reinvented. When a writer becomes published, the new identity of being an author can be daunting. Running with that identity accomplishes the reinvention state.

- Think for yourself. Don't always run with the pack. You don't want your reinvention to be the same as someone else's reinvention. This is one place where it can be all about you! Think thought leadership.

- Experiment and explore. This is part of the previously discussed notion of evolving. New information leads to new thoughts. New thoughts lead to new ideas. New ideas lead to reinvention.

- Trial and error is just fine. Not every reinvention idea will work. Starting over can be frustrating but starting with a new idea is starting over in another form. That's just fine.

- Recognize the wins and successes. Reinvention doesn't necessarily have an endpoint, it is a process. That means there won't be one major, end of the line celebration that says you won the reinvention race. Recognizing wins, successes, and accomplishments along the way, though, is vital to keeping the reinvention fire stoked.

Accomplishing these finer points of reinvention can be significant contributions to the transformation of any business, organization, or life. I'm sure Franklin lived these principles even though he hadn't had the benefit of reading this book.

In case you haven't noticed, Apple® has reinvented the electronic retail industry. They were successful at reinventing technology and now they are reinventing the electronics retail business around the world. Their no-pressure sales and service are based on many five star hotel concierge models.

Apple returned to its core; doing what they did best. They didn't just do technology right. They didn't just issue new software applications and products. They offered ease of use and a total experience—two guiding points of their recent and continuous reinventions. Have you ever seen an Apple user read the instruction booklet that comes with products? Probably not, ease of use make instructions less important.

Apple is in the process of creating an Apple Community. Witness an Apple store grand opening. It looks like a pep rally complete with cheers, cheerleaders, applause, T-shirts, and more. During the normal course of Apple's business, workers just hang out and dispense information; no hard selling here. Sharers of information sell more than sellers of products.

To say that the stores are aesthetically pleasing and the wide variety of products is completely accessible is a complete understatement. Just go visit one and tell me if your jaw dropped wide open upon entering. Add to that free use of products, applications, free Wi-Fi, free advice, and tutorials; and Apple has created a whole new meaning to the reinvented brand experience. Apple stores have been reinvented into tourist attractions. This position is perfect in the age of rampant consumption where desire-driven markets are focused more on wants than needs. Having once only appealed to artists, graphic designers, and renegade computer nerds, Apple consumers now run the gamut from students to executives as the many "i-devices" appeal to age, income, and professional demographics of all kinds.

To Reinvent Is to Innovate

The basis of this successful reinvention is without question its ability to innovate. Innovation is definitely a recipe for reinvention. Innovation in Apple's case is often referred to as a "thought factory." If you want to do your own Apple-style reinvention; innovate, modify anything and everything around and within you. Make it interesting, tell the world about it, and celebrate it in grand style. Think experience. That's what Apple does. Just watch.

Brand experts suggest that successful companies of all types and sizes should reinvent their image, identity, and brand periodically, if not often. Anne Mai Bertelsen, Founder and President of MAI Strategies, a marketing consulting firm specializing in integrated marketing strategy development and implementation, offers another definition of reinvention: the act of making something already invented, like it was the first time, whether in a different form or another. She used this definition to introduce companies that reinvented to overcome the worst recession in recent decades.

Following are a few of her observations.

Dogfish Brewery chose to produce beers that reference the wine world: revealing and marketing a brew's recipe lineage or explaining how ingredients affect the beer's "nose." Dogfish products are introduced in experimental or extreme fashion. Liquor De Mot, a bottle of conditioned malt liquor comes in its own brown paper bag. Non-standard ingredients have been used like green raisins in their brand, Raison D'être. These ideas support the reinvention of the beer world. In the late 90's, Dogfish turned the heads of beer consumers by introducing a beer series labeled as Ancient Ales. Ancient Ales beer recipes were created using the chemical makeup of residue found in pottery and dishware from various archaeological sites.

Dogfish Brewery brand of draft beer, Verdi, Verde Good, has been produced and served green since 2005. Its color came from brewing a Dortmunder style beer (a pale golden lager made popular in the 19th century in Dortmund, Germany, this style of beer exhibited a classic clean character with hints of biscuity malts. It contained spirulina, a blue green algae—gross sounding but definitely reinvention at work. These and brands like Chateau Jiahu, Midas Touch, Olde School Burleywine, and Altar Boy reinvented Dogfish Brewery manufacturing.

Sometimes reinvention can be achieved with just a simple viewpoint. Bertelsen reported on ING Direct, USA, a savings bank offering savings, investment, and lending services to Main Street USA customers. Their simple yet mighty reinvention came when the company researched the retail banking experience and offerings. ING thought about what the real banking experience would look like from the consumer's point of view. This new perspective created endless possibilities of products that the reinvented ING Direct could offer. Just like Apple, ING's focus on experience resulted in a reinvention.

With the auto industry hit hard during the recession of 2009, many companies were forced to reinvent. Many chose to revisit the offering of a value priced model. In other words, price was being modeled as a differentiating purchasing factor more than ever before. Audi stepped back and took a look at what the notion of luxury meant in recessionary times. They found that luxury was no longer all about private prestige but rather about public consumption of purchasing and owning a well-known brand standard. This doesn't sound like much but it played out in all of Audi's ensuing marketing, resulting in a significantly better sales performance than their competition. Although sales declined 10 percent, performance was still better than the competitive brands that declined close to 30 percent for the recessionary year.

With these instances and cases in mind, businesses should be quick to note a few lessons:

- Connect consumers with the product or service and the whole brand experience. Let their stories be told not only by the marketer but also by the consumer. Social media marketing and Web 2.0's user generated content is allowing the consumer to have a voice.

- Learn from mistakes along the path of reinvention and don't be afraid to reinvent the reinvention, adjusting along the way.

- Break out of conventional wisdom and thinking. This also means stepping outside traditional business models and practices, especially if they are declining or flat out not working.

- Invest as heavily in the actual act and process of reinvention as you would the marketing of the reinvention.

Domino's® Pizza chose the milestone of their 50th anniversary to announce their reinvention. Domino's President Patrick Doyle said, "There comes a time when you know you've got to make a change. The fact is, we love our pizza, but as times change, so do consumers' tastes. We've created a pizza product to reflect what consumers are looking and asking for."

Domino's Pizza undertook an 18-month-long reinvention process that included their product and their brand promise (brand experience). From mid 2008 to 2010 (just before the heaviest pizza day of the year, Super Bowl Sunday), they changed 80 percent of their menu. Focus groups were used to find out exactly what consumers were thinking as well as to provide insights into what pizza they were or were not purchasing. Domino's stated that the product/brand reinvention was inspired partially by monitoring consumer comments and conversation about their brand in social media networks and communities. The reinvention also had its own website, www. pizzaturnaround.com. Their response to what they heard was a new recipe: new crust, new sauce, and new cheese—a complete reinvention of their product.

The reinvention emphasis was based on quality as well as its more well-known service attribute. Since its inception, Domino's has been known for great delivery. Their original mission statement was, "hot pizza fast". With the reinvented pizza they want to be known for great delivery *and* having the best tasting pizza. Hot pizza fast, sells. So does the best tasting pizza.

Their quality promise is backed with a full satisfaction guarantee. Sometimes, during the course of reinvention, bold unconventional moves have to be made. The guarantee states that if there is not complete satisfaction with the pizza experience, they will make it right or refund the customer's money. Notice the emphasis on the brand—pizza experience.

Reinvention does not always come cheap. In the case of Domino's reinvention, a six-week ad campaign at the cost of $75 million was undertaken to tout its reinvented product and brand. This was in addition to spending over 200,000 hours retraining workers at all of its U.S. stores.

Domino's reinvention was summed up by Chairman and CEO David Brandon when he stated that the reinvention was the biggest product introduction they've done, since, "well, pizza."

While reinvention has been discussed related to brands, companies, or businesses, it also applies to individuals like you and me. This book is provided for your business and/or your life with the hopes of reaching a wider audience desiring more than they have now. So how does reinvention apply to people? Can reinvention consist of a few tweaks about how you go about life or is it more significant, requiring complete personality and character makeovers? Many say both are required for effective reinvention but others take just one path.

To many, reinvention is a process more than an event or series of events. This process, many times, is a work in progress. Some will say that reinvention takes place when changes are needed. But those who are the most accomplished and happiest will say that reinvention takes place when changes are wanted. In the case of Benjamin Franklin, he wanted change all the time. In the entrepreneurial world, more so than the structured corporate world (reinvention is what moves entrepreneurs from idea to idea, business creation to business creation, and career to career. Entrepreneurs are always pursuing dreams, achievement, and success. Reinvention prevents complacency. Reinvention prevents one from becoming out-of-date. Reinvention can redirect those on a path to failure to a path to success.

Some treat reinvention as part of life and the pursuit of happiness and do so, not just often, but continuously, just like Franklin did. Life happens and has to be dealt with. That is a fact, but sometimes life throws curveballs. We've all seen them and all have had to deal with them. Life also consists of things we don't like or want and things we definitely want changed. Reinvention means making things different for a better life; handling these curveballs so that things improve and changing to get what we want. Call it life, call it growth, or call it a work in progress. Reinvention can make a better you. And that's where the whole process starts—with you. Figure out what "you" are all about, what drives you, what your dreams are, and what your make up is. This is your first step in your own reinvention.

Then take the less than desired parts of your analysis and work towards making them more desirable, better, and most of all, positive. Using that as your foundation to build on, watch for and capture the opportunities to reinvent. Use the opportunities to build on top of that foundation toward your dreams, hopes, wishes, and aspirations. Whatever your foundation, life requires that you adapt, rework, change, and reinvent. Never look back. Always reinvent.

Sometimes It Takes a Crisis

Sometimes it takes tough times like a poor economy or a personal obstacle to provide an incentive for people to reinvent themselves. Economic downturns leave many with a desire to find new paths to survival and abundance. These new paths show up and are created in the form of reinvention.

During a late 2009 survey, in the middle of economic turmoil, Opinion Research Corporation found that 72percent of the Americans they surveyed, agreed that, "as a result of their experiences during the financial crisis, they need to reinvent themselves and enhance their earning power…"

Matt Fageness, a former Kansas State University professor and avid reinventor, credits education as "an absolute fundamental" in making any change or reinvention. He has gone so far as to classify students and those wishing to reinvent into three categories:

1. Those who want a career in a particular industry and realize they need to learn more to achieve and succeed.

2. Those who have found themselves in a hard spot financially because of downsizing or a declining industry.

3. Those who have an acceptable career but ultimately want to do something else.

In view of this, McKinsey, the management consulting firm, has shown that during recessions, individuals are willing to spend more on their education..

You have options in life. You have the ability to choose the paths you take. You can be like everyone else—the norm—or you can pursue your deep down, gut-level passions and lifelong dreams. Reinvention is not necessary for the norm, it is for the passions and dreams. Reinvention hit home in the world of Hollywood stardom with Reality TV star Vicki Gunvalson. Gunvalson is an entrepreneur, mom, workout fanatic, wife, author, clothier, and a star on the reality TV show, "The Real Housewives of Orange County." Needless to say this full life needed to be organized and prioritized and even at its fullest, it also required reinvention. Working with a life coach to rebalance, Vicki boiled down her much needed reinvention to just a few points:

- Focus on Vicki the person
- Focus on Vicki the professional
- Have a Sense of Purpose
  - What do you want in life?
  - Why do you want it?
  - What are you going to do to get it?

Sometimes even the fullest of lives need reinvention. A little bit of focus, prioritization, and balance can reinvent the fullest of lives into one that is filled with happiness and even greater purpose.

Pret A Manger, a British fast food chain, has always strived to be on the progressive side of reinvention. Founded in 1986, Pret has aimed to elevate expectations about what fast food can really be. Their reinvention insight is that you can organize a mass market business around innovation rather than standardization. In one year the company introduced 111 new items to its menu while retiring just as many. Their own brownie recipe has been reinvented more than 30 times in pursuit of perfection and in response to changing consumer demands. Company management understands and endorses the fact that they challenge conventional wisdom. That's a classic approach to reinvention. The Sunday Times of London has listed Pret A Manger as one of the top companies to work for in Britain. They are the only restaurant chain, fast food or otherwise, on the list, a true testament to the constant process of reinvention.

The real poster child for reinvention is Samuel Langhorne Clemens, better known as Mark Twain. Clemens was a serial reinventor driven mostly by money. Vowing to never again live in the childhood poverty he experienced as the result of his father's failed business ventures, Clemens sought more money by continuing to reinvent his ventures and career. In addition to the earnings from his primary career as an author, Clemens earned great wealth developing numerous inventions and forming a major publishing firm. He invested his profits wisely and continued to increase his skill at investing over the years. Throughout his life, Clements was a cocoa planter, a riverboat pilot, a prospector, and a journalist. He reinvented his journalism career by becoming a professional speaker, booking a manager, and traveling the country. He even ventured into stand-up comedy performances. He not only reinvented himself, he reinvented the businesses he was involved in. For example, he hired sales representatives to sell the memoirs of Ulysses S. Grant to booksellers using a script he had written and turned the book into a best seller.

Clemens's success at reinvention was his ability to identify an opportunity, develop it, revise it, modify it, and take full advantage of it. Although his reinventions involved risks, he knew the rewards were his as long as he made the right investments of time and money and delegated work to people he could trust.

Wrapping up Reinvention for Businesses

Here are some actions you might consider when reinventing your business:

- Gear your mind for change and don't think about the way things were in the past.

- Look for buying trends and sell them to consumers. You might have to do research to find out what people are buying.

- Sell what customers already want from your inventory of products or services.

- Ask your customers what they need that no one else is supplying.

- Don't look at change as up or down, good or bad, new or old. Understand and accept that things are just different.

- Market what your product does for your customers rather than what the product is all about. Take advantage of advances in technology as quickly and often as possible, be a market leader instead of a follower.

- Find out from customers what your company is doing that they really like and do more of that.

Ask customers to tell their stories about their great experiences with your company.

What can you do that they can tell others about?

Find out how to satisfy the people who spend the most money with your company.

I close with the perspective of Rebecca MacDonald, the founder of Cogent Communications and a freelance writing professional who writes The *Serial Reinvention* blog: (http://serialreinvention.com/)

"…not everyone has to narrow their focus in order to be successful. Or even happy. Some people are, by nature, serial reinventors. Opportunists. We're interested in many things, and our curiosity can take us in many directions. This is mostly frowned on by the 'pick your passion' crowd, not to mention prospective employers who value long-term loyalty over the more difficult job of keeping their employees engaged and challenged.

"I think it's time we started debunking this notion that you have to "pick a passion" to the exclusion of all else, and begin encouraging dabblers. I think maybe we should envision our careers not as ladders, but more like those rock walls you see in climbing gyms. There are many paths you can take up the wall, with numerous footholds and toeholds along the way. Sometimes you even have to back up a bit, or go sideways, to find the path."

Reinvention is a never-ending process. It's the daily, ongoing pursuit of personal growth and fulfillment—a path that ultimately leads to more rewards and greater responsibilities.

Backing up, going sideways, or finding a new path are all part of reinvention. Which direction will you go? What does your new path look like? What will you look like reinvented?

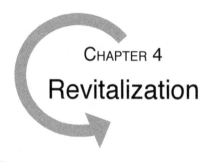

CHAPTER 4

Revitalization

REVITALIZATION – HARLEY STYLE

I drive through Milwaukee frequently travelling from Chicago to northeast Wisconsin. One early summer day, I noticed an unusually high volume of traffic. The operative word here is unusually. The unusual part was that the majority— yes the majority—of the traffic was made up of motorcycles, specifically Harley-Davidson® brand motorcycles. What I thought was hundreds of bikes turned out to be thousands, literally. I wondered aloud what was going on. I'd passed the Harley headquarters on this same stretch of highway, many, many times. Were they all headed to the Harley headquarters, I wondered? Then I spotted a banner with the message, "Happy Birthday Harley," draped over buildings. Being a marketer I was impressed. I was impressed even as a lay person and a non-Harley enthusiast. I subsequently researched and found that in 1984 there was a similar event with just 28 participants. Now the fest-goers approach the 200,000 number. What has happened since 1984 to cause such resurgence? The answer was the pumping of new life into a brand; the realization of the power of a Re word in action: Revitalization.

I later found out that the make-up of the sizeable crowd was very diverse, including factory workers, CEOs, athletes, farmers, and teachers. Harley's revitalization effort touched a lot of people including many new target markets for them. Between 1984 and now, Harley-Davidson motorcycles became "cool." It was cool to be part of HOG—the Harley Owners Group®. Motorcycle and merchandise sales have skyrocketed since then. Prospective purchasers were put on waiting lists.

Communities of Harley enthusiasts sprouted up all over. The creation of this community—950 HOG chapters worldwide— was the secret to this brand revitalization. Big businesses and small businesses alike can do the same thing, especially with the surge in social media marketing.

 Harley Owners Group Mission (www.hog.com)

"Your mission—if you choose to accept it—will be a simple one: To Ride and Have Fun."

That is the mission of the Harley Owners Groups; the HOG mission.

Here is what Harley says is the "bottom line:"

"We like to think of Harley-Davidson, from the top corporate officer to the newest Harley owner and rider, as one big, happy family. The Harley Owners Group helps us turn that philosophy and mission into reality."

"Does that sound like something you want to be a part of?" That's what Harley puts out as a question to owners and enthusiasts. If so, then they encourage any and all to join HOG. They go on to say, "You'll ride, you'll have fun. Mission accomplished."

That is how Harley built a community and a following. Similar tactics can help you build a following and community. Building both are ways to revitalize a brand.

In the business world brands are born, brands mature, brands plateau in terms of popularity, acceptance, and awareness, and eventually many decline and die. This certainly is not the case with every brand but is common. When the demise occurs, companies face a decision: let them die and go to the brand graveyard, put more life into them, or launch new ones.

Many times the investment required to launch new brands, new products, and new services can be cost-prohibitive. When this is the case, revitalization of dying brands is the more attractive path. To begin revitalizing a brand, investments of time and money must be redirected to major marketing campaigns associated with the revitalization. The objective is to raise awareness with past customers as well as with new market channels urging them to purchase products again or for the first time. Revitalization of a brand may involve:

- Subtle changes in product, identity, packaging, or service delivery

- Drastic changes in product, identity, packaging, or service delivery

- Complete overhauls/makeovers that change a brand experience in every respect

Samsung Brand Revitalization

Ted Mininni is president of Design Force, Inc., a metro New York area consultancy that specializes in brand identity, package design, and consumer promotion campaigns for the food and beverage industry and the toy and entertainment industries. He writes the brand papers column of brandchannel.com in which he said that Samsung® went through major brand revitalization in the mid 1990's.

Samsung decided to go from commodity electronics producers and distributors to developers of innovative product designs and retailers of an eventual global brand. This could only be done through revitalization. The attempt was successful because of the focus on product innovation and brand design strategies that were put in place. Samsung became known as, and branded as, a product innovation leader in their industry. Competition took notice, consumers took notice, and the trade took notice. In the 2005 Interbrand and Business Annual Report on Global Brands ranking, Samsung was rated as the 20th most valuable brand among the world's top 100 global brands, assessed at a worth of close to $15 billion. Now that's revitalization—a billion dollar revitalization!

Brand revitalization remains a strategy for many brand managers. And the strategy gives new life to a dying brand when it is perceived as mature, aging, tired, and dragging. Revitalization of the brand along with rejuvenated packaging and marketing brings the message to its target customer base. A revitalized brand builds favorable equity that ends up right on the bottom line of a company's balance sheet. Just check out Samsung's performance.

Revitalization Is Also a "Healing Art"

Sandra Gray of Milford Healing Arts understands the importance of revitalization. It is part of her business's service offering which is described on her website, www.milfordhealingarts.com, as "Energy Balance." Sandra states on her website that, when we are born our bodies have an almost inexhaustible flow of vital energy. With age and stress, we begin to slow down and stiffen up due to deficiency and stagnation in this natural energy flow. The body's healing energy continues to maintain physical function and resist illness. Adjustments are sometimes needed to prolong optimal health.

She goes on to state that more than 4,000 years ago, Chinese doctors discovered that there are internal pathways in the human body, like invisible rivers, through which all energy flows. They called the energy Qi (chee). These doctors devised techniques to supplement the energy flow when it was weak, drawing upon deep reservoirs stored in the body. They also learned how to remove blockages and relieve pain. This is the science of acupuncture. Acupuncture techniques worked well along with natural plants, which the Chinese compounded into herbal formulas and mineral therapy, creating therapeutic combinations that strengthen the internal organs returning them to healthy functioning. This is a revitalization art.

Today, these ancient revitalizing techniques are available with modern enhancements to help restore a normal energy balance to the human body. Sandra Grey of Milford Healing Arts knows this and so do her revitalized clients.

Whether a business or the human body, revitalization can be a significant tactic and approach to bettering yourself, your business, your brand, or your livelihood. Most entrepreneurs, most business people, and most human beings strive for excellence in all that they do in life, in work, and in play.

Your Steps to Revitalizing Your Life and Business

1. Concentrate on the moment; be in the present.

So many times our minds are pre-occupied with the past, the future, or the worries that go with those times. Preoccupation interrupts the mind's ability to concentrate and its ability to pump new life and vigor into the moment. Concentrating on the past is a distraction. Revitalization is not oriented on the past. There is no way you can revitalize what has already happened. You have to consciously think about the moment at hand for revitalization to occur. You can't think about the phone call you had 10 minutes ago, the movie you watched last night, or a website you wanted to tell your friends about. Revitalization occurs when you think about what you are doing and experiencing right now. It's being more aware of your actions and thoughts, and what your senses bring in to what you are doing. If you are writing a letter, an email, or communication of any kind, concentrate on it. Pour your heart and soul into it. Be the letter. Feel it. Don't allow distractions of the past or even the future to enter your being. Get rid of the preoccupation, close it out, compartmentalize it in your head. Think about the here and now and focus. Appreciate the present opportunity and don't wander from that thinking. Period. Make the moment come alive. This is a revitalized state and it will expand as you let it expand. All the senses can expand with revitalization. Accept it, appreciate it, and fuel the revitalization.

2. Open yourself up to inspiration, motivation, and education.

I know this sounds like motherhood and apple pie, but an attitude of lifelong learning will go a long way. Lifelong implies a continuity of this attitude and approach to business and life. Use your resources, your network, and your mental attitude to drive you to the next step you desire. Make a list of inspirational experiences you have had. Document what has motivated you. Document what will motivate you in the future. Look for the common denominators that inspire and motivate you, and apply them to all you do. Continuous learning means continuous revitalization.

3.   Slow down and savor.

Realize the good in you and the good in any work you do. This represents a positive viewpoint and realization. Become fulfilled with this realization. Don't let today's hectic schedules distance you from opportunity and from giving thanks for your opportunities. The more you savor, the more you are fulfilled, the more you will want that feeling of fulfillment to continue. Sometimes this means slowing down. Part of slowing down is relaxing. Whether it is a physical activity that relaxes you or a mental activity or particular state of being, make time for what relaxes you. You can do it. We all have the same amount of time: 24 hours every day. Prioritize the time, make the time, feel it, enjoy it, appreciate it, and breathe. You will feel revitalized. Guaranteed!

4.   Don't let perfection distract you.

This is one of my favorite beliefs and one that has let me and the people I work with accomplish more, feel fulfilled, and especially feel revitalized. Good enough may be good enough. Life is too short to get hung up on those things that that suck the life out of us personally and professionally because they are just not 100 percent perfect. You can revitalize without reaching perfection.

5.   Replenish your energy.

Since the definition of revitalization is to pump new life and vigor into something, replenishing your energy is a revitalization technique. Relaxing has already been mentioned related to revitalization but replenishment of energy can come in the form of a nap, exercise, reading, writing, a healthy meal, or even a drink (alcoholic or non-alcoholic).

 Re words and Re principles work together.

Consider the following:

The State of Florida reported that the governor signed a bill to "revitalize Florida's economy." While the word revitalization was used throughout the bill, the details only claimed renewal and the bill itself was designated as the Community Renewal Act.

Florida realized that one of the keys to renewal was revitalization, breathing new life and vigor into its current economy.

Not only are past customers awakened with revitalization but a revitalization effort will create brand awareness with new market channels and new target markets.

Customer needs and wants continuously change, competition comes from all directions. There are always new consumers who have never heard of past and dying brands. A revitalization effort can change that.

The National Hockey League attempted brand revitalization by going the "identity" route. After a year off due to a major labor dispute, the NHL evaluated the identity that had been in place since 1918. In this case, identity refers to who they are and what their fans think of them when hearing or seeing their "brand." The NHL redesigned their logo and updated it to show a 3-D image with a metallic look to represent Lord Stanley's trophy which some say is the most coveted championship trophy in all of sports. Lettering and typefaces were changed to suggest speed and quickness. This professional sports league was trying to pump new life into a look that was tarnished over time and especially by the recent alienation of fans.

Cadillac® also jumped into the Revitalization Game. Ted Mininni, president of Design Force Inc., stated that the Cadillac brand was dying due to lack of consumer relevance. Cadillac revitalized their brand by going the route of new products. The Escalade was introduced with plenty of features that appealed to new fans and old aficionados alike. Backed by a heavy promotional campaign to new and old target markets, Cadillac differentiated itself from other leading automobile brands. Cadillac returned to icon status with a strengthened brand within a restructured General Motors® Corporation.

Consumer products sometimes go through more than one revitalization effort. Increased brand competition, changing consumer and market preferences, and demands from the number of repackaged and new products hitting the retail shelves all call for more frequent revitalizations.

 Rededicated Mission = Revitalized Brand

Brand revitalization usually starts with a rededicated mission as a base; a rethinking of a company or product direction (notice the continued use of Re words). When General Tire® started down its path of brand revitalization, management clearly stated that "the new elements represented its new branding message of progressive products that were technology driven with an emphasis on utility."

You can bet there were many conference room hours spent by senior management kicking this around, brainstorming, visioning, and getting this platform ready for revitalization. General Tire went on to say that their identity and logo changes represented "… a significant milestone in our company's history and symbolized the strategic transformation underway for the new General Tire." General Tire had a revitalization plan. In addition to a revitalized brand they continually add a variety of new products, extensive new advertising, and promotional campaigns. They also communicate consistent brand and marketing messages. It all started with their rededicated mission.

Pyramid Brewing Co. of Seattle also used mission brand philosophies and corporate culture shifts in their brand revitalization. They stated, "As a craft pioneer, Pyramid is extremely passionate about our brewing and we are continually inspired by the cities where we brew, live, and play every day. We believe we have successfully distilled that enthusiasm into our beer and our new packaging. To remain relevant in a landscape with greater variety, we believe we must constantly evolve our brand and Pyramid is committed to providing craft consumers with interesting beers and experiences that quench their thirst for adventure."

It is clear from these examples that revitalization in business is a process of focus and vision that do the following:

- Agrees on a company mission, a rededicated mission and/or vision to back the brand. A new mission or vision or slightly changed one is the basis for revitalization.

- Determines, based on customer research if it is available, what brand components need to be changed:

  ◆ Name

  ◆ Logo

  ◆ Colors

  ◆ Typeface

- Investigates and improves where necessary, the brand experience including service, ease of buying, and loyalty.

- Advertises, promotes, markets every step and component of the brand, its repositioned message and any new mission or cultural shift linked to the revitalization that is relevant to the target market.

Revitalization Is an Outward Portrayal of New Energy

In 2005 Red Lion Hotels, a hospitality and leisure company primarily engaged in upper-mid scale, full service hotels, undertook a five year aggressive growth plan to expand into 100 new markets in new cities. Revitalization of the brand was a major component of the aggressive growth plan. They launched the revitalization as an "outward portrayal of new energy."

Revitalization step #1 was to change the corporate name from West Coast Hospitality Corp. to Red Lion Hotels Corp. This was a direct effort to focus on the Red Lion Brand. Sometimes revitalization starts with just knowing your focus. This provided vision and direction to their revitalization. At the time Red Lion associated the word rejuvenation with their new brand identity. In this case, a brand rejuvenation was the basis for expansion that led to a revitalized company.

Certainly in Red Lion's case, brand rejuvenation was not the only component of revitalization. Red Lion also elevated its product and service standards. They introduced innovative marketing programs and state of the art technology compliance training tools. They also improved hotel quality and comfort. The response to the revitalized company was that customers and prospects noticed the changes and responded positively, measured by increased hotel revenue, quarter to quarter.

Red Lion Hotels clearly stated that their vision for revitalization was that they wanted an excellent product, a well recognized brand, and world class systems to help position them to more aggressively pursue growth and partnership opportunities. Today Red Lion Hotels face the same economic challenges that many other consumer related businesses do, but they still stay focused and aggressive on branding and rebranding programs, products, services, and the company as a whole. What started out as rejuvenation and revitalization continues as a core business philosophy and direction.

Stay the Same and Die or Revitalize and Live, Grow, and Prosper

Whether you are a business, an entertainer, a professional, a parent, a college student, or an average Joe cruising through life, revitalization thoughts have crossed your mind. You may not have recognized them as such, but they have. This usually occurs after a crisis, a period of complacency, or too much lack of purpose or drive.

As a business or a person, there are several revitalization components that lead to success and well being:

- Be different – Sure, this is easier said than done for many. In business you often hear about the Unique Selling Proposition or the differentiating characteristics or even a competitive advantage. If you're complacent or lacking success, it may be time to differentiate. If you are already successful, revitalizing your differentiating features could lead to new levels of success.

- Offer New Value – First, have a good product or service that your business offers. Revitalization requires offering new value. New value starts with and grows from a solid product / service base.

- Offer New Value to New Recipients – In business this is aiming for new market channels or new target markets. On a personal level it's making new friends, expanding your networks, and joining new communities.

- Communities – Let people know about your revitalization. Market a business in new ways and market your revitalization. Talk to people about your effort to revitalize your life and your life's direction. If you're already successful then talking positively about revitalizing leads to ongoing revitalization, ongoing success, and new levels of fulfillment.

In 2005, AT&T® began its first day as the largest telecommunications company by introducing a revitalized corporate logo. At the time, Edward Whitman, Chairman and CEO of the new AT&T, stated that AT&T's shift to a new brand and new look symbolized the strategic transformation of the new company. He first stated that the revitalization efforts reflected the fact that while the brand had a long and proud heritage, the "attributes that bring the company to life are as fresh and new as ever." Chairman Whitman added that, "The revitalized market symbolizes innovation, integrity, quality, reliability, and unsurpassed customer care."

Just one quick word of caution: Understand the costs associated with brand changes, logo changes, and revitalization in general. When AT&T changed their logo, they had to change the branding and logo application on:

- 50,000 company vehicles
- 6,000 company buildings

- 40,000 sets of uniforms for AT & T representatives
- 40,000 hardhats
- More than 30 million monthly customer bills and statements

So how do you revitalize a business or organization efficiently and effectively? That same question parallels the question, how do you revitalize your life, your persona, and everything else about you? The reason these two questions are parallel is that businesses and organizations aren't things. They are groups of people with common interests working towards a common goal. Revitalized people lead to revitalized businesses and revitalized organizations.

A business doesn't have an attitude, the people working in it and customers being served have the attitudes. Businesses aren't smart or talented; the people working in them are. Businesses don't need to be optimistic, enthusiastic, and customer-oriented, people do. So the answer to the two parallel questions is the same: revitalization requires revitalized people. This means creating a people-related spirit of optimism, enthusiasm, success, positive environments, and more!

Here is your revitalization checklist as one of these people:

- Segregate the pessimists, eliminate them or don't let them dominate your time. Spend time with optimists.
- Have control over conversations and thoughts and keep them positive.
- Take positive actions: create, communicate, and celebrate them.
- Improve. Make "getting better" a lifelong goal, a habit, a mindset, and a way of life.

- Don't worry about the past or about things you cannot control. Take positive action to overcome your worries before they overtake you. Sometimes this means doing things you don't like or don't feel comfortable with. Having it behind you, completed, done, and over with is a far better feeling that more than overcomes the worry.

  ◆ Adapt the attitude to live life a day at a time. Plan for the future but live today to its fullest.

  ◆ Find ways to improve your physical energy but don't let it overtake and dominate your thinking:

  ◆ Exercise your body consistently

  ◆ Eat right

  ◆ Exercise your brain consistently

  ◆ Take deep breaths (take one now while reading this)

  ◆ Rest and relax

  ◆ Take breaks

  ◆ Take vacations

  ◆ Sleep

  ◆ Pay attention to all things physical and realize that your physical well being is a part of revitalization.

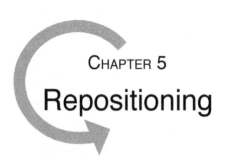

CHAPTER 5

Repositioning

Repositioning is a strategy for life or business that arises simply from the desire for something different from what you have now. There is an old saying, "If you always do what you've always done, you'll always get what you always got." Along the same lines, one of my favorite quotations is, "Nothing changes if nothing changes." It sounds simple but like a lot of things related to improvement it is common sense but not common practice.

If you don't make the decision to change, if you don't change the way you live your life, you will never feel better or achieve the happiness and fulfillment that you strive for. Things may change, but the change may not be the one you want. Heraclitus knew the concept of things always changing when he said "You cannot step into the same river twice."

Repositioning to Attract Voters

Companies and other entities reposition brands, products, strategies, and vision to achieve new objectives. Take the Republican Party for example. According to the experts, if they are to win further elections they will have to reposition their brand. This is done often in the political world, especially after a defeat. After the 2008 election, Gallup polls showed a decreasing favorability of the Republican Party brand and a positive trend for the Democratic Party brand. Of course, the popularity of both parties will continue to change, thus requiring constant analysis for the proper positioning or repositioning.

Repositioning can take many forms. Consider the following:

- Many companies, organizations, or products start with a logo change to reflect modern times, especially if the current one appears to be outdated. This is often the start of a repositioning effort. Along with the logo change comes a change in the basic marketing messages and the vehicles to communicate those messages, such as a revised website, new print materials, new style of radio and TV media, and so on.

- Involving new generations is often an objective of repositioning for companies and organizations. This is certainly the case in this political example. Get rid of the "old men," Republican identity. Appealing to young voters and minorities with a new identity and refreshed platform would help reposition the Republican Party.

- Repositioning can happen when you emphasize the differentiating characteristics of a new brand. While this is true in all of marketing; people need to understand, now more than ever, why a new brand is better and preferred and what the new brand experience could be.

- More effort is needed to appeal to target markets. This is a key marketing fundamental and also key in repositioning. "Joe the Plumber" almost repositioned the Republican brand to attract the average and ordinary "Joe," but lost its momentum. The jury is still out as to whether Sarah Palin can accomplish what is needed to reposition the brand of the Republican Party.

- Repositioning needs a concentration on and communication of the right message. If the message and platform are not perceived as worthy; repositioning will not be accomplished, regardless of how their marketing or political campaigns are constructed.

Repositioning to Attract Market Share

In the book, *Positioning: The Battle for Your Mind*, authors Jack Trout and Al Ries discussed the fact that marketing messages must find an empty, comfortable slot in the consumers mind. Repositioning could be defined as finding an empty, comfortable, and available slot in the consumer's mind. But that was thirty years ago. Trout is now quick to point out that times have changed. Competition is more fierce. Consumers are more savvy. Communications are faster when once-successful companies are in crisis mode, repositioning becomes important to survival.

G Re-po-si-tion: transitive verb – to put into a new or different position

---

Repositioning in business is a viable strategy that can be an urgent, competitive reaction to ensure survival. In this case, repositioning applies to a whole company, not just a shift in product lines or brands.

The battle for that consumer mindshare is fought daily in the marketplace. It is literally up for grabs every day. Sometimes preferences change because a competitor effectively repositions the current market leaders out of the consumers mind. The competitor grabs that newly available mind slot for itself. This is not done by bashing the competition but by directly engaging the consumer about value thus improving the consumer's perception of your brand.

Gary Ryan Blair is the President of The Goals Guy, a highly focused training organization whose mission is to help clients build and sustain superior performance. Blair is the author of the best-selling book, *Everything Counts! 52 Remarkable Ways to Inspire Excellence and Drive Results.* His book is a definitive guide on excellence and its call to a greater awareness of its impact. His website describes Blair as "… a visionary and gifted conceptual thinker. As one of the top strategic thinkers in the world he is dedicated to helping his clients win big by creating focused, purpose-driven lives." Blair has quickly become known for his blog entitled "Invent New Rules or Die." He offers what he calls a serious message for people who want to prosper in today's economy. And guess what? His message involves a degree of reinvention.

Blair states that the revolution in information and communication technologies has fundamentally and permanently altered the domestic and international business landscape. I'm not sure I agree about the word permanent, especially after my research for *Re The Book*. But his main point is that one of the most far-reaching consequences of these changes is a massive shift in the competitive balance of power. Blair states that for the first time in the history of commerce, five person boutiques can take on multinational giants and win. He goes on to say that, "It's going to get tougher to generate competitive advantage by simply doing the same old things a little bit better. Technological changes have ushered in an era of radical repositioning. Competitive advantages and profits will belong to innovators who transcend the existing parameters of competition. Strategic repositioning forces competitors to play by the new rules of the game, rules that you, yourself have largely devised."

Here are the three varieties of strategic repositioning he offers on his blog (for more, visit: http://www.everythingcounts. com/invent-new-rules-or-die-2/):

1. Create an entirely new industry.
2. Reinvent how an existing industry operates.
3. Set the world standard for an emerging industry that others are creating.

I would add: Reevaluate your position related to each of these three strategies constantly to see whether you are behind, on top, or breaking through.

Consider this repositioning: today, consumers believe that even though chemical fertilizers work well, they still are potentially hazardous to our environment. Green solutions and organic products are all the rage as a result of repositioning. Organic product concepts have been strategically placed in the minds of consumers as being safe to use: The Organic Safe Alternative to Chemical Fertilizers is a repositioning statement, planting (no pun intended) a solid concept in the mind of prospects and customers.

In recent times, investment banking firms Goldman Sachs and Morgan Stanley shifted from investment banking to commercial banking. The expectations of all stakeholders, including clients, employees, and shareholders, needed to shift.

The company needed to influence this shift and all related perceptions and reposition the entire company.

Small to medium sized firms are in the same boat, especially in tougher, recessionary business climates. Business strategies and positioning that happens in better economies often become ineffective, requiring businesses to reposition. Companies selling to affluent markets reposition to emphasize value.

Repositioning is not always a complete overhaul of thoughts, promises, marketing messages, and related communication but often a "nudge" or redirection towards the same goals or objectives using different strategies and tactics. Repositioning is often a recognition that the consumer has changed, that markets have changed, but the company has not totally changed.

Sony® used repositioning strategies to guide the success of their PS3 video game system. What once started out as a "media hub," was repositioned as a "game system" and is now being loudly touted as a "total entertainment solution." Notice this repositioning was not a complete overhaul of the product's delivery but a redirection towards the same goals and objectives with different strategies, tactics, messaging, and communication. This was substantiated in an interview with the L.A. Times, where Sony executive, Peter Dille, stated, "We have been a game company for years and we would never walk away from that, but research confirmed there is a larger proposition under our nose. We wanted to reposition as a total entertainment solution. We felt like we can really own entertainment."

Guinness®, brewers of the best-selling alcoholic drink of all time in Ireland, Guinness Stout, repositioned by changing their tagline from, "Bring It to Life," to "Good Things Come to Those Who Wait." Taglines position a business or brand, and new taglines can be one way to reposition a business or brand.

What Guinness did with these taglines, according to Paul Cornell, marketing manager for Guinness, was to reposition the brand from one to be enjoyed at a "low tempo" occasion—people drinking on their own or with a handful of people to a drink enjoyed on "mid-tempo" occasions; get togethers with four or five friends. The Irish stout was to be repositioned as a drink to be enjoyed at home among friends and families. Their repositioning had as an objective to drive those who love the brand to drink it more on relevant communal occasions such as while watching sporting events.

Guinness was trying for new target markets in view of shifting spending patterns during recessionary times. New target markets are generally the initial impetus for repositioning. Did it work?

Guinness didn't completely overhaul their direction. The repositioning slightly nudged the product to different target markets. They still maintained their connection with sport and related teams and events but repositioned as a nudge to the market place in mid-tempo fashion.

Personal Repositioning

We all begin at different starting points: rich, poor, educated, uneducated, healthy, sick, friendly, depressed, and so on. There are limitless levels of personal growth and development open to everyone. To attain points different from the starting points described and to realize the growth and development mentioned, repositioning has to happen.

The famous motivational and inspiring pastor, T. D. Jakes, uses many Re words to describe repositioning yourself. He states, "If you don't like the way your life is going, redesign it. Redeem the years you lost. Restore your vision. Revive your passion for living and Reclaim what was dormant inside you." That can be the effect of repositioning!

One area where repositioning is quite evident in everyday life is in the job search market; specifically, repositioning career paths in the direction of a new interest or on a new path to survival. In today's economy, layoffs are prevalent, downsizing is in the news, and companies are shutting down at a higher rate. With all this come displaced and dislocated workers who are then forced to look at other industries and companies that are hiring.

Considering a new career is a foundation of repositioning for you. Understanding your true interests, inside and outside your comfort zone, aids in the reevaluation of new career paths and of your life's repositioning. While it can be intimidating and scary, repositioning yourself can be highly rewarding if you prepare and do your research properly—research not only about the career but about yourself.

Here are a few repositioning tips and challenge questions on pursuing careers outside your past area of concentration and experience:

- What industries interest you?
- What positions are available in the new industries that you are interested in?
- What strengths and talents can you use to reposition yourself for a career path (even though it might feel awkward at first)?

Once you've answered these questions then move on to:

- Research specific companies.

- Network and seek a mentor in the newly chosen area of concentration.

- Determine and communicate how your previous experience and skills would transfer or be applied to a new position.

- Communicate honestly. It's OK to state that you are repositioning for something new.

- Be enthusiastic, interested, and interesting.

- Just as with any new career endeavor, be persistent.

Repositioning takes on many connotations. From a branding standpoint, repositioning helps a brand capture a consumer's mind and offers a new experience in a new and different way. An updated brand, as a result of repositioning, reflects a change in the consumer's perception and experience. Perception is positioning. New perception is new positioning or repositioning. Taking a brand to a new "perceptive" level is a deliberate attempt to attract a different target market or to reinvigorate past consumers.

Bob Gorman of Mahan Rykiel Associates offers strategies to reposition resort properties for success in recessionary markets that can be applied to other businesses and industries. Consider the following Gorman strategies:

- Engage marketing professionals to do an "experience" audit. This includes understanding strengths, weaknesses, hidden opportunities, marketing position, and image profile to provide a basis for a repositioning strategy.

- Play up unique and authentic attributes, much like a unique value proposition. This includes understanding the competitive advantage and current market perception (positioning) so that a "new" place can be created or perceived.

- Create an online advantage and presence to cater to new target markets that are predominantly online and then use websites more to offer a clear and repositioned identity.

- Approach the "guest experience" with special nurturing to bring back customers for repeat businesses. Businesses can be repositioned in the mind of current customers just with different attention.

While repositioning is often referred to when strategizing for businesses, products, services, and brands, the same thought process and approaches can be done to reposition for life. Think with the end in mind. Ask the questions, "What does that 'repositioned life' look like? What will be the perception that others have of that 'repositioned life?'"

Just look at all the successful people around you. They typically don't keep their successful positioning by doing the same things over and over again. They always change something, do something in a different way, try something new or head in a different direction. That is the essence of repositioning for success. Many people are always looking for something new or a new direction so that they stay fresh and current instead of stale and out dated. You have to take note of all your experiences, learn from all your mistakes and successes from each position you hold, and apply those lessons to new positioning—repositioning. This is the foundation of consistent success that is the desired end result of repositioning.

CHAPTER 6

Rejuvenation

To rejuvenate means to make young or youthful again or to give new vigor to. Rejuvenation can also refer to restoring to a new state, like rejuvenating old cars or rejuvenating a brand or product in business.

Many tales, stories, and myths tell us about the quest for rejuvenation. In ancient times it was believed that supernatural, magical, or mystical powers could bring back youth. These thoughts prompted many to set out on adventurous journeys to find that elusive rejuvenation. Some sought potions. Some sought a fountain. Others sought icons. An ancient Chinese emperor actually sent out explorers seaward to find a magical pearl that would rejuvenate him.

The quest for rejuvenation scientifically reached its height with alchemy. All over Europe and Asia alchemists searched high and low for mythical substances. Take note of the Philosopher's Stone, the mythical substance that was believed to turn lead into gold and to prolong life while restoring youth. Although alchemists failed in their search, they did pave the way for scientific thought, study, and methods that eventually led to some of the medical advances we enjoy today.

Rejuvenation stories continued well into the 16th century. In the 16th century many expeditions were undertaken to find the Fountain of Youth. Famous Spanish explorer Juan Ponce de León led the expedition around the Caribbean islands and into Florida to find the elusive fountain. Led by rumors and conjectures, the expedition continued the search and many perished. The Fountain was nowhere to be found.

New Life and Vigor

Rejuvenation for business can take the form of simple new tasks, an in-depth analysis with a resulting plan for change, or a total overhaul or makeover. Any one of these is a lot! When any rejuvenation project is executed, new blood pours into the business, bringing new life and vigor. Rejuvenation can bring new life and vigor to an individual as well.

Businesses cycle, products cycle, and people cycle—some cycles follow the simple pathway of birth, maturation then death. Others are up and down, sporadic and not consistent. When businesses cycle down, or are in decline, new life is needed to reverse the decline. This new life is rejuvenation.

In tough economic times and recessionary markets and conditions, businesses still need to innovate. Innovation is a form of rejuvenation. Tom Peters, the revolutionary, forward thinking sales guru and futurist, presented his thinking on the subject in his controversial writings, *Innovate or Die!* Peters stated, "It's pretty simple. The truth is we know nothing about what the future may hold for American business. The only mortal sin in such an environment of uncertainty is to do nothing."

Businesses that don't innovate, especially in declining markets and tough times, are vulnerable and exposed to great risk. Most businesses realize this but not all of them do. Consumer demands change, tastes and styles expire and grow stale, and technology impacts all businesses. Product life cycles shorten. Products pass the mature phase and enter the declining phase. Passing the declining phase means death to a brand, product, and even a company. Throw in the new affects of global competition and companies and businesses have to stay on their feet constantly, monitoring product and market life cycles.

Innovation Can Lead to Rejuvenation

On the flip side of no innovation is obviously those companies and businesses that take innovation seriously. Innovation and the introduction of products and services can counter product maturation and decline but still have associated risks. Close to 40 percent of all new products fail. Companies lose significant money on these failed introductions. Texas Instruments® lost $600 million in the home computer business. Remember RCA's videodiscs? That only cost the company $575 million. Think about the Edsel…more significant losses.

The conclusion to innovate or not to innovate is that doing either can be risky. To remove some of the risk, businesses turn to rejuvenation. Thinking back to the definition—rejuvenation re-introduces or restores to a new state. Rejuvenation also breathes new life into those products that have hit the mature point on the product life cycle and have already started the decline phase. Rejuvenation strategies can help a business regain lost market share and revive the revenue stream while producing profits.

In 1994, Nestle® decided to revive two of its recently acquired candy brands: Raisinets and Goobers. For fifty years those products were mainstays, primarily sold only in the nation's movie theatres. Nestle reformulated the products, redesigned the packaging, changed the distribution patterns and made them into national brands

Barbasol® shaving cream, once sold in tubes and jars, was a product category leader until the 1940s. The product continued a typical life cycle ending production in the early 1950s. Enter Pfizer, in the 1960s. Pfizer bought the company and established Barbasol in the typical aerosol form that we know today. They marketed the product as a "value" label in supermarkets. In return for these efforts, Barbasol rose into the top five aerosol creams by 1979. By 1985 Barbasol had captured the number one spot—rejuvenation at its finest.

Nike®, Kmart®, Toyota®, Sony and American Express® have all been involved and will continue to be involved in brand rejuvenation just like Apple, Raisinets, and Barbasol. Innovation is an important part of each of these companies' missions and that results in rejuvenation. These companies and others like them realize that old brand names carry tremendous value in terms of brand equity. Creating new brand equity is expensive, takes much more time, and still carries the risk mentioned earlier. This brand equity, available for rejuvenation, exists because the brand has developed an emotional bond with the consumer.

Age Prevention

Rejuvenation strategies are considered to be advantageous to new product/service introduction. But entering new, unfamiliar, and uncharted territory can be costly.

Familiar "old brands" can result in lower promotional costs for rejuvenated products and brands. Some equity can be less expensive to promote than no equity. Rejuvenated products can be created from old, dying products at a fraction of the costs that brand new product development incurs.

Not only are promotional and developmental costs lower, rejuvenated products can reach markets faster than newly developed products. Vendors and channel partners are already familiar with old products. Less time means lower costs which translate into higher profits and higher business reinvestment—and even sometimes survival.

The same goes for fighting for consumer mindshare. New products have to break consumers' recognition barrier whereas rejuvenating old brands bypass this step.

At some point in their lives, brands get tired. They get old and some even die. According to the American Marketing Association, 80 percent of all new brands fail. Images and identities stay the same and new and younger brands move in, clearly an aging problem. One way to overcome this problem is with rejuvenation, synonymous with "age prevention." Brand rejuvenation is more than repositioning. It encompasses a wider communication effort including increased advertising and marketing in addition to the repositioning strategic considerations.

Rejuvenation is not repositioning. Take Wal-Mart® for example. Wal-Mart management tried repositioning away from low prices with a move towards higher end and higher priced products. They signed endorsement deals with pop music stars, Destiny's Child and Garth Brooks, ran expensive ad campaigns in high end magazines, and even rolled out a fashion runway event at New York's highly-touted fashion week. Wine offerings and jewelry products went high end. Wal-Mart tried to reposition at a higher end. That was their definition of rejuvenation. Management forgot what made the brand famous and successful along the way. Their repositioning had no credibility and failed.

As a result executives looked back on what had made the Wal-Mart brand famous. They returned the company to its roots. They looked at all the things that went right when the Wal-Mart brand was at the peak of brand popularity. Once all that was "reestablished" they then took a hard, serious look at what changed pertaining to consumer demands and preferences, and what they needed to react to. The result of this rejuvenation effort was their campaign, strategy, and direction, "Save money, live better." It's clear that they revisited "what got them to the dance," which was low prices that saved customers money. The rejuvenation factor was the emotions of their customer base that would use the money saved to spend on "living better." Market timing was on their side. As markets trended downward, middle and upper class consumers entered the world of money-saving shoppers. This was classic rejuvenation and these markets reacted with a favorable response.

Rejuvenated brands play on nostalgic sentiment while developing new identities that emerge and capture, once again, their dominance in a new world of competiveness. Nostalgia sells and can remain a part of rejuvenation. Consumers who recognize old brands have a higher sense of reliability, quality, and trust with the perceived longer life span.

With all Re words, many definitions apply. Whether it's to make new again or to breathe new life into something, the Re prefix is powerful. It opens up new direction and changes for the better. Whatever the definition inference, it is usually positive.

Rejuvenating anything can be patterned after the hypothetical age reversal process. Reversing, rather than stopping or preventing the aging process, requires repairing or replacing what has been damaged by aging. For a business it might mean new people, new products, new brands, new strategies, or a brand new vision.

Science tells us that there are no natural laws to prevent the repair of damaged cells, tissues, and organs that are part of aging. Many scientific experiments have involved repairing and replacing the loss of hormones that cause aging.

Our options today for rejuvenating the body involve cosmetic and aesthetic changes to individuals to create a youthful appearance. Cosmetic surgery of the human body typically involves the removal of wrinkles and fat, and reshaping sagging body parts. The result is a new appearance that seems to slow down aging.

Rejuvenation and the fight against aging has fueled and birthed an entire industry of vitamins, lotions, cosmetics, drinks, and exercise equipment. Rejuvenation often refers to being young again. Becoming young again has been the subject of movies, books, stories of all types— spiritual, and non-spiritual. In the 1924 movie, *Vanity's Price*, actress Vanna Du Maurier is restored to her pristine loveliness of days past and is described as having a "youthful change in her whole nature." She becomes a "dazzling creature who basks in the sunshine of flattery." Who wouldn't want that kind of rejuvenation?

Thinking Your Way to Rejuvenation

Rejuvenation can happen also within your mind. Think about the following things and the affect they have on your mind. Will you become young again, fresh again, adapt a new mindset towards something, or rethink something as a result of these? If the answer is yes, put them on your rejuvenation to-do list:

- Watch a funny movie.
- Watch a positive emotional movie.
- Read a less than serious book.
- Read a humorous book or a feel good story.
- Relax your mind—think about that.
- Listen to soothing music.
- Look at pictures of friends, families, and happy times or events.
- Experience silence.
- Clear the mind of toxic thoughts.

A conscious commitment to rejuvenation is essential to growth, creativity, health, well being, and happiness which all lead to a more successful, fulfilling, and positive life. For more tips to rejuvenate your business or life, consider or do the following:

- Surround yourself with people who are healthy, happy, positive, and young-at-heart.
- Start thinking consciously about the whole concept of rejuvenation. Even if you have a few false starts, you will, at some point, break through with rejuvenated thoughts, a plan on how to keep it going, and strategies to always be rejuvenated.

Try something you've never tried before. Read a new genre of books, listen to a new genre of music. Explore a new interest. Experience a new activity.

- Start the day off positively and take "positivity" breaks.

- Eat well. Treat yourself to something decadent from time to time.

- Exercise. But don't overdo it or put pressure on yourself to exercise. Do it as a break. Take exercise further only if you want to.

- Work and play hardest during your most productive part of the day. It's different for everyone. Some people are morning people; others are night owls. Do the most at your best and favorite time.

- Create the new, don't rehash or dwell on the old, especially if old thoughts and ideas bring back bad or negative memories.

- Make a list of rejuvenation tactics and brainstorm for more ideas.

- Meet new people. Introduce yourself to people you normally wouldn't talk to. Try it in the grocery store line, at the health club, on the bus, at the theatre, or in a restaurant.

- Take breaks, even days at a time, from television viewing, Internet surfing, and cell phone talking. Even stop reading books and newspapers as a break. When you do this have a notepad close by. Write down happy thoughts, ideas, perspectives, and even questions. Keep it as positive as you can.

- Outline, map, or plan ideas and aspirations. Connect the dots and find associations; dig deep with detail.

- Spend time around children, act like them, look at the world through their eyes, talk to them, and listen to their ideas.

Why are these activities relevant to rejuvenation? Rejuvenation, by definition, is becoming young again in mind, body, and spirit. It is reversing the aging process and staying young. This brings the peace of mind that comes with being free of sickness, pain, and suffering. Rejuvenation means being able to do all those things you did when you were young, fit, and more energetic. Taking this thought process and these feelings a step further, this all suggests that being young and innocent, open, honest, and free of harsh judgment are related benefits of any rejuvenation.

Is all this rejuvenation easy? If it was, everyone would do it and the whole world would be happy. It's not easy, but everyone can do it. Every single individual possesses the power within to change and to change for the better. Everybody can benefit from change, but many resist it because it isn't easy. It takes a commitment. Commitments aren't easy to keep.

Commit to rejuvenation and your world will be more peaceful and you will be in a better place.

CHAPTER 7
Reengineering

Author Nanette Turner was interviewed about her book, *Re-Engineering Your Life to See and Seize Opportunities*, on a Long Island, NY, talk show. During the interview, she described reengineering as tweaking something for the "best optimization." Turner went on to relate reengineering to her hobby of sailing. She stated that when you are under sail and you want to optimize the wind, you become aware of the direction and intensity of the wind. You watch the tell-tags on the sails to determine if you need to let the jib out or crank it in, or adjust the traveler on the main to get the best the wind has to offer, constantly reengineering. She closed her interview by saying that we can all use a little tweaking now and then to get the best wind behind our backs as we sail through life's challenges. "Being in control and focusing your life in the direction that makes you passionate about your life is the goal," Turner says. How to get there takes reengineering—sometimes constant reengineering like Nanette Turner's sailing experience. Today, the newest reengineering buzzword is not necessarily redesign it is optimization as Nanette Turner describes.

Making Improvements Toward "The Way It Should Be"

So far, in our discussions about Re words, the words improve, change, and making things better keep coming back. Consider and note these same concepts and thoughts as related to the reengineering of life and business.

When you think of reengineering a life or a business, you should first think of what the situation is, then what the situation should be, and what parts need changing to get to that "should be" state. That's exactly what a doctor does when he attempts to improve a patient's health. The same goes for a business that wants treatment from the "business doctor," or manager. The manager assesses existing business processes then plans changes for improvement and better business health in the spirit of Nanette Turner's sailing optimization.

Sci-Tech Dictionary defines reengineering as "the application of technology and management science to the modification of existing systems, organizations, processes, and products in order to make them more effective, efficient, and responsive." Reengineering in business has been described as a management approach aimed at making improvements. The same can be said for reengineering a life. Dr. Phil uses the words "change" and "new" when talking about reengineering life. He stated "If you're living beyond your means, it may be time to reengineer your life. That means more than making a few changes or altering a few priorities. It means you question everything and look at your life in a whole new way."

The decade of the 1990's was known as the decade of reengineering in business. Business process reengineering was one of the biggest business ideas ever. It was described in many books, featured in articles in all the top business publications, and a popular topic of business conference keynote speakers. Reengineering was present everywhere businesses turned. During this heyday, reengineering was known to include things like redesign, workflow improvements, process improvements and efficiencies, unreasonable expectations (stretch goals), and taking things apart to put them back together differently and better.

In some cases reengineering went hand in hand with "downsizing," and "rightsizing." Pacific Bell® announced in 1995, that it was cutting 10,000 jobs because of "reengineering." Shortly thereafter, Apple (then known as Apple Computer) did the same, using the same Re word as its justification. Anyone involved in continuous improvements, systems engineering, or process improvement soon became engaged face to face with reengineering, whether they used that term or not. Businesses were reengineered tirelessly. Sometimes they were successful; sometimes they weren't. Many managers soon realized there was also a people aspect to process improvements. Those who didn't failed in their reengineering efforts and abandoned reengineering projects.

Disrupting Status Quo

In their book *Reengineering the Corporation*, authors Michael Hammer and James Champy defined reengineering as, "the fundamental rethinking and radical redesign of business processes to achieve dramatic improvements in critical, contemporary measures of performance, such as cost, quality, service, and speed." It is almost like throwing everything out the window and starting over; starting over with a blank sheet of paper for redesign, rethinking, and renewal.

One of my favorite reengineering descriptions was in a 1994 article entitled, *How to Make Reengineering Really Work* by Eugene Hall, James Rosenthal and Judy Wade. The authors said, "When companies reengineer, there is a disruption of status quo." So, it follows that when individuals break out of one comfort zone on their way to another one, there is a disruption of the status quo as well. They must have had a premonition about *Re: The Book*. (See Chapter 9 on challenging the Status Quo).

Think about what you see or experience all around you related to reengineering; related to a fresh start:

- A salesperson wants to sell more merchandise than last year. What reengineering of approach, tact, and targeting, will be necessary?

- A runner wants to beat last year's time. Is it enough to continue run the same way, hoping for a faster time? Remember, hope is not a reengineering strategy. Reengineering a workout, training plan, or fitness management plan?

- A driver wants to beat traffic on the way to work will take a reengineered route.

- You as a golfer try to beat your best score. How can you reengineer your swing or putting to significantly improve?

- A student strives for better grades. How will reengineered study habits lead to more As?

So whether it is for your business, your job, or your life, what major change do you want to happen that will challenge the way you always do things? What do you want to reengineer?

Take It Apart and Put It Back Together, Better

Reengineering recognizes that larger processes or situations are made up of smaller parts, sub-processes, and components. When engineers want to know how a piece of machinery or a process works, they take it apart and study and understand the individual components that make it work. In the vernacular, this is known as reverse engineering. Reverse engineering can aid reengineering. Take apart the item or process, look at the contributing parts and make changes to reengineer it to something new. Modern day reengineering in this sense is often referred to as a "mashup;" a term first associated with the mixing and remixing of music and now associated with anything broken up and put back together, especially anything technical.

Wikipedia® offers the following information related to mashup:

- Mashup (digital), a digital media file containing any or all of text, graphics, audio, video, and animation, which recombines and modifies existing digital works to create a derivative work

- Mashup (music), the musical genre encompassing songs which consist entirely of parts of other songs

- Mashup (video), a video that is edited from more than one source to appear as one

- Mashup (book), a book which combines a pre-existing text, often a classic work of fiction, with a certain popular genre

- Mashup (web application hybrid), a web application that combines data and/or functionality from more than one source

Continuous improvement, breaking records, hitting new goals all involve learning from what others do and applying it to your own situation; taking bits and pieces from another's success and putting it together into a workable solution for you, your situation, your style, and your abilities—a real human mashup.

A word of caution is offered here. Put your knowledge into action. You can gather all the facts, education, information, and knowledge that you can from reverse engineering and compile it, sort it, and organize it, but unless you do something with your new knowledge, the same thing happens, nothing new is accomplished. Be actionable. Don't confuse research with activity.

Make your list of what you want improved and what needs reengineering. List your models that you want to "mashup" and reengineer your way to all new levels.

Reengineering certainly was present before the 1990 buzz. In the early 1980s, new Taco Bell® CEO John Martin devised and implemented a major reengineering effort for the company. Martin reengineered to increase the quality of Taco Bell's products while redesigning time spent in food preparation, paperwork, and the overall management of the food preparation process. One system redesign was creating a system in which food was prepared in central commissaries and shipped to kitchen-less restaurants, a clear reengineering. The central commissaries cooked the meat, prepared the beans, and chopped the cheese and vegetables. These ingredients were then shipped prepackaged to each individual restaurant. The reengineering allowed the firm to improve the quality of its products, reduce chopping accidents, save on preparation time, and reduce store space, resulting in a $7 million savings per year, at the time. Sales now are approaching $2 billion and the savings as a result of that reengineering still continues.

Fast forward to today. Is there still a place for reengineering? The answer? Absolutely—in both business and life. Businesses should address, across the board, processes and practices from time to time. The same thing applies to your life. Sometimes this "addressing" could mean a serious kick in the pants in order to reach new levels; aggressive reengineering. Throwing out broken processes and removing "less than best practice" procedures is needed. Whether used aggressively in complete makeovers or used in moderation in incremental improvements, there is a place for reengineering in business and life.

Rework and Redefine

Here are a few cautions to consider along the reengineering route and a few tips for reengineering best practices:

- Reengineering requires a change in "thinking."

- Reengineering involves risk, especially if radical changes are needed to deliver new results or if desperation sets in.

- All those involved in reengineering--whether company, corporate, or personal -- must be totally committed to the process. There will be resistance or forces that push back at anything new. Efforts still must continue relentlessly until all efforts are given a chance.

- Have a reengineering plan, set reengineering goals.

- Technology, manufacturing, and processes are just a part of reengineering. People factors need to be considered, too. Look at everything related to the reengineering including the effects of change on all people, all being influenced and all influencers.

- Understand that reengineering can be time consuming. Give it time. Don't give up.

When considering reengineering, study what others are doing that you want to do. This works whether you are reengineering your company or your life. Adopt the effective techniques that others are using and rework those methods to fit your circumstances, situation, or style. Understand that it is OK to ask for help, tips, or new ideas from those involved in the same process. For example, use the Steven Covey principle of starting with the end in mind when considering reengineering. Think about what you want and work backwards, defining the steps along the way. Implementation then moves forward as you complete the defined steps.

Goals for reengineering can sometimes take the form of a big target. Quantum leaps are acceptable. Don't be confined by too much talk of "incremental change" associated with reengineering. Reengineering often requires big change.

It's always best when doing something new, whether it is a reengineering effort or a rejuvenation effort to approach things with a success mindset. Hope is not a strategy.

So how do you go about reengineering? I'm glad you asked. Consider this reengineering plan:

1. Set targets and have overall and/or detailed objectives.

2. Have a vision as to how targets can be reached and objectives can be achieved.

3. Communicate the vision and the priority to all involved and/or affected by the reengineering.

4. Analyze the current situation in depth and in detail.

5. Recommend changes for improvements starting with small steps that lead to achieving the larger overall goals identified.

6. Implement the changes.

7. Continue with the changes relentlessly and consistently.

8. Reassess to see how the changes are contributing to the overall goal.

9. Tweak your plan as needed until you reach your goal.

That's it. That's all there is to reengineering. Reengineering your life means that you are in control of your life and you can take it where you want to go.

CHAPTER **8**

Rethink and Rejoice:
Pursuing Personal Happiness

Improving your life, just like improving your business, is a process that many have referred to as a journey. Most of us want to make the process or journey the best that it can possibly be. So far, the ideas in this book have mainly applied to businesses and organizations. But they can be applied to your life, too, because businesses and organizations are groups of people working toward a common goal. Businesses don't have attitudes, the people working in them do. Businesses aren't smart or talented; the people working in them are. Businesses aren't enthusiastic or optimistic; the people in them are. When Nationwide Insurance® ran network TV commercials to start the new millennium, their slogan was "Life comes at you fast. How well prepared are you for what life throws at you?"

The Pursuit

As you prepare for life's challenges, remember that there will be hurdles. Yes, there will be obstacles and yes, there will be curveballs thrown your way. Whatever is thrown at you has to be dealt with. Your ability to handle the challenges is key making the journey as pleasant as it can be. Making the journey pleasant is analogous to the never-ending pursuit of happiness.

Most of us associate the word pursuit with the phrase, "pursuit of happiness," as written in the Declaration of Independence: "We hold these truths to be self-evident, that all men are created equal, that they are endowed by their Creator with certain unalienable Rights, that among these are Life, Liberty, and the pursuit of Happiness."

According to Benjamin Franklin, "The Declaration of Independence only gives people the right to pursue happiness. You have to catch it yourself."

George Bernard Shaw stated, "This is the true joy in life—the being used for a purpose recognized by yourself as a mighty one; the being thoroughly worn out before you are thrown on the scrap heap; the being a force of Nature instead of a feverish clod of ailments and grievances complaining that the world will not devote itself to making you happy."

Happiness comes to fired-up people, to cause champions, to those whose zest for life is glowing and apparent. You see them in all walks of life. You know who they are. You can spot them a mile away. That happiness is contagious. Happiness breeds happiness. Become that champion. Get fired up about something. Pursue your own happiness with zest and don't watch time amble by in the form of the ticks of a clock or the sunrises and sunsets. Mark Twain certainly realized this when he stated, "Whoever is happy will make others too."

An interesting post on Facebook® recently stated, "…life is seriously filled with surprises and they are stressing me out! Slow down life and let me breathe!" The basic translation of this plea is, "If I didn't have to deal with certain things, I'd be happier."

The suggested solution here is to learn how to avoid things that make you unhappy. Perhaps this is an obvious statement, but well-worth taking to heart and practicing.

How you react to what life throws your way is in your control. This reaction is usually a result of how you think. The thinking point is your opportunity to turn a negative experience more positive or to ignore it altogether. It is your opportunity to not let full-on negative emotions carry through to a negative response, reaction, or feeling. Adjust your mindset. Yes, I'll say it again. Adjust your mindset. You are the only person who can do that, and it is totally in your control. Spend a bit more time in the thinking phase and you will be on your way to less negative energy and fewer negative thoughts. The result will be forward movement to more positive thoughts, actions, and happiness. Choose your level of happiness by choosing your thoughts and your thinking process. Better thinkers are happier people.

Whatever problems, challenges, obstacles, or mind blocks you had at the age you started thinking about your happiness, probably still exist today regardless of your age. It's funny how these challenges never seem to go away, yet people become happier as they age in many cases. The key is finding what's best about you that will help manage the less than desirable challenges that could overpower your happiness. Managing challenges helps prevent unhappiness.

To truly live a happy life is to be passionate about life and all the opportunities it affords us. How many times have you viewed people waiting for the good life to drop in their laps? How many times are people just watching the clock of life pass aimlessly? If you don't make passion a way of life, you will hate to get up in the morning, hate your job, and waste away with an unfulfilled heart. You will be unhappy. Passion about anything contributes to happiness.

Get Excited About the Possibilities

Another approach and similar to adopting a passion for life, is to get excited about the possibilities. Make a list and itemize possibilities and opportunities that would excite you if you realized them. This fulfillment will certainly make a happier you. Possibilities can arise when you meet new people. Every person you meet provides an opportunity to learn, grow, and contribute to the passions for life, for you, and for them. This is known commonly as personal growth. Those who invest in personal growth invest in change, renewal, rejuvenation, and reinvention. As a result, I believe they realize happiness.

If you leave this book with nothing else, I encourage you to leave with the notion that happiness is a choice; your happiness is your choice. You can choose to feel good or choose to feel bad. Yes, it can be that simple. Your real mindset should be to feel right in your current circumstances, consistent with your own wants and needs. Think about it. Thinkers are happier.

Many people are unhappy because they constantly compare themselves to others. Reengineering your mindset to eliminate these comparisons will contribute to your happiness. I realize that it's easier said than done but so is a lot of life. In the spirit of Nike, "Just do it!"

List five things that make you happy:

1.

2.

3.

4.

5.

List five things that make you unhappy:

1.

2.

3.

4.

5.

Knowing what makes you happy and unhappy is the key to being able to manage the dual challenges of eliminating unhappiness and creating happiness. Once you've figured that out, develop, follow, and live the entries on the list that make you the happiest. Eventually, those specific activities will become habits that will help you keep your own happiness alive. It is important to make the effort to be happy. Sigmund Freud said that unhappiness is a default condition because it takes less effort to be unhappy than to be happy.

Studies from 2005 and 2006 show Americans were no happier than they were 50 years ago despite significant increases in prosperity and wealth, decreases in crime and pollution, larger living spaces, better lifestyles, and better overall quality of life. University of Minnesota researcher David Lykken offers an explanation, saying that happiness is 50 percent genetic. The other half is choice, determination, and intention. Abraham Lincoln said that, "Most people are as happy as they make up their minds to be."

Psychologist Mihaly Csikszentmihalyi, former head of the Department of Psychology at the University of Chicago, is known most for his studies in happiness and creativity. He theorizes that one route to happiness comes during playful or creative activity. Csikszentmihalyi's work is part of a branch of psychology that has become known as positive psychology. Wikipedia states that positive psychology is a recent branch of scientific psychology that "studies the strengths and virtues that enable individuals and communities to thrive." People have been discussing the question of human happiness since, at least, ancient Greece.

Psychology has been criticized as primarily dedicated to addressing mental illness rather than mental wellness. Several humanistic psychologists including Abraham Maslow, Carl Rogers, and Csikszentmihalyi developed successful theories and practices that involved human happiness. Despite the lack of solid empirical evidence at the time behind their work, these psychologists chose to emphasize phenomenology and individual case histories that led to developing positive psychology.

Another recipe for happiness comes from research psychologist and author of *The How of Happiness,* Sonja Lyubomirsky. She states that individuals who are happiest make lists of things they are most grateful for, practice random acts of kindness, forgive their enemies, notice life's small pleasures, take care of their health, practice positive thinking, and invest time and energy in friendships and family. Which of these do you do regularly?

Rules of Happiness

The past is past; you can only go forward, pursuit implies future, ongoing activity.

- Lighten up; some things are just not meant to be taken seriously.

- Good enough might just be good enough (OMG! The purists and the perfectionists just stopped reading here, but that's OK).

- If it's not good enough, make something happen to make it good enough.

- Happiness is meant to be shared. Share it but remember it's your pursuit, not someone else's.

- Your happiness alone can make others happy.

- Happiness is meant to be enjoyed; unhappiness is to be managed.

Roadblocks to Happiness

The following roadblocks will definitely stand in the way of your pursuit of happiness:

- Worrying about what others think.

- Comparing yourself to others.

- Not having a mindset of "continual pursuit."

- Inactivity – the experts say that emotional well-being is tied to physical activity.

- Choosing an "I can" or "I want" mindset.

- Listening to the complainers.

- Fearing mistakes or the negative consequences of mistakes.

- Having a perfectionist attitude.

- Being exposed to negative, unhappy situations, such as violent movies, arguments, yelling, and so on.

Creating and practicing a set of specific habits and activities is one of the best things you can do to increase your happiness. Identifying roadblocks will help you realize what contributes to your unhappiness.

There is the age-old debate of whether or not money can buy happiness. Social psychologists and related pundits offer the perspective that says that the true resolution to debate is that it is a function of the person and the related psychological factors.

Being satisfied with your life's direction and the related fulfillment that comes from it really happens when activities consume you to the point where you forget about you, when you erase the thoughts related to time pressures, and stop worrying about the negative. Try this: Immerse yourself in a happy activity and feel its satisfying richness. Let go of the negative influences and the emphasis on material things. Check your happiness level. Do what you love, and you will be happy!

One of the happiest people I have ever met was a factory worker, twice my age at the time, who couldn't read or write but could figure his paycheck amount to the penny. This man was very proud of his factory work, his contribution to a team, the product that was made, and the concrete result of his efforts. He was active and very happy. His activity made him forget the negative influences in his world. His mindset controlled his happiness. Anyone can do this.

Throughout this book you have read that your life's direction is a function of your choice. To be happy, you have to make a choice to undertake and engage in the activity that makes that happen. You have to be motivated towards becoming happy or being involved in the activity that leads to happiness.

Let's look at some ways to achieve happiness:

1. Don't let the highs last, don't let the lows linger.

2. Feel as good as you can physically. If you don't feel good physically, do something about it.

3. Surround yourself with positive, optimistic, and encouraging people.

4. Surround yourself with influences that inspire you.

5. Be hungry for more happiness at the height of your happiness.

6. Be intentional with your desire to be happy.

7. Smile, laugh, and mess up your hair. Get a can of silly string, for crying out loud.

8. Appreciate those things or situations that provide your happiness now.

9. Realize that you, and only you, are in full control of your decision to be happy.

10. Know what's best for you and stick to it. No one else knows what's best for you.

I included this chapter about the pursuit of personal happiness because I think that happy people make happy, more productive workers. Revitalized, reinvented, or rejuvenated people lead to revitalized, reinvented, or rejuvenated businesses.

Greg Easterbrook, author of *The Progress Paradox: How Life Gets Better While People Feel Worse*, states that research shows that people who are grateful, optimistic, and forgiving have better experiences with their lives, more happiness, better health, and higher incomes. It is no secret then, that the happiest people have reengineered their lives to include as much contact as possible with family and friends. They have rejuvenated themselves by immersing themselves into their own pleasurable daily activities and they have an internal compass that leads them to do what is right for them.

Michael Neil, author of *Feel Happy Now*, lists a few benefits of making the choice to be happy:

- Happiness feels good. Our bodies have a natural predisposition towards pleasure (good feelings) and away from pain (bad feelings). This is a biological survival instinct, and is governed by the oldest parts of our brain. Given the choice between a perceived pain and a perceived pleasure, your brain will take you towards the pleasure and away from the pain every single time.

- Happiness makes you healthier. When "happy chemicals" are released into your body, your muscles relax and all your neurological and physiological systems return to their natural state.

- Happiness leads to success a lot more often than success leads to happiness. The clarity of thought and easy flow of inspiration and intuition that accompany good feelings in your body make it easier to make the choices that lead to success. They also make success fun.

No matter what is going on in your life right now, no matter what the past has dealt you, it is very possible to feel happy right now. No one can be happy 100 percent of the time, but you can achieve high levels of happiness a high percentage of the time. It's not just in this book; it's in your head, Happiness is a mindset; it may need to be reinvented once or many times over, to achieve the level of happiness you want. By reinventing, repositioning, reengineering, and revitalizing your mindset, I think you can become happier today than you were yesterday. Here are my favorite ways:

- Write down what makes you happy.

- List 10 things in life you are grateful for.

- Tell yourself, "It's OK to make mistakes."

- Look around. Notice things. Notice things that make you smile or bring happiness to you. Use all your senses.

- Give something to someone.

- Do something new or different or even challenging. Imagine your happiness when you accomplish the feat.

- Avoid bad news or conversation about bad news.

- Do your best.

- Smile. I know it's corny but it works. Try going to sleep with a smile on your face. Think happy thoughts when going to bed.

- Live consciously and intentionally.

- Tell people what you really think, especially family and friends.

- Take a break and think. Turn off the lights. Turn off sound. Think in peace.

- Pay it forward; pay someone else's toll or parking.

- Dance or sing when alone. Yes, it's a stretch but try it. I guarantee at least a smile. It's like laughing out loud.

CHAPTER 9

Reconsidering the Status Quo

Challenging the status quo is a slight departure from an actual Re word but the underlying concepts, strategies, and objectives are very similar to many Re words.

Coasting Can Cause a Crash

In the mid-nineties, business author, Judith Bardwick, darn near scared secure employees out of their wits with the release of her book, *Danger in the Comfort Zone - How to Break the Entitlement Habit That's Killing American Business.* Those who read it hoped that their bosses didn't get anywhere near the book. The purpose of the book "…was to examine the phenomenon of the entitlement mentality in the American workforce—people's preoccupation with their rewards rather than their responsibilities."

Bardwick went on to state that people felt entitled to rewards and were lethargic about having to earn them. Motivation and job satisfaction were low. Fear caused people to feel paralyzed; the threat of layoffs made them focus on protecting their jobs rather than doing them well. She also noted that people were energized by a challenge that noticed and rewarded accomplishments and behaviors. Challenges and rewards were driving forces that helped break people out of their comfort zone.

Since the 1995 book, Bardwick has pointed out that although the "fear" element has undoubtedly grown in the last few years, the entitlement attitude is still firmly entrenched at all levels.

Most people know their comfort zone well, either at work or in their lives, since they spend or have spent a lot of time in it. Why? They spend time there because it's safe, it requires little effort to stay there, and there is little or no risk of failure. These factors all produce a "coasting" atmosphere. Security and comfort can be a good thing unless something changes.

Change can disrupt comfort. That is the danger referred to in the title of Bradwick's book. Change can scare the daylights out of some people. That fear can be a limiting factor in all that you. That feart can chase you right back to the comfort zone, never to realize your fullest potential nor fulfill your happiness goals. Your comfort zone represents the status quo.

Comfort zone, complacency, or just good enough; call it what you want. You can stop at any of these plateaus; but how many times have you wondered about having more, doing more, being happier, or being acknowledged and recognized? Remaining at status quo is contradictory to change. Status quo will hold you back from changing and realizing or obtaining more of what you want; more of your potential.

Breaking Through Status Quo

Terry Little, a program manager for the Department of the Armed Forces, stated in the newsletter of The NASA Source Project Management & Engineering Excellence that people clinging to status quo resent change. This is often the case in companies and organizations of all types, but especially so in government where there seems to be an aversion to managerial risk.

In government there is often a greater premium put on not failing than there is on truly doing something better. Is this any way to grow, progress, or move things forward? Is this any way to break through the status quo? Ronald Reagan said that status quo was Latin for, "…the mess we are in." Politicians talk status quo all the time as they profess changing from it.

If the status quo is unacceptable to you, pay close attention to the following and implement and practice accordingly:

- Identify opportunities for improvement in your business, job, or life. Write them down.

- Don't debate about whether your plan is a good idea. Focus on the results.

- Spend as much time planning the implementation of change as you spend thinking about what needs to be changed.

- Persistence pays off if you try to change the status quo. Persistence shows you have the courage to change.

- Repackage your ideas, solutions, or actions until they are accepted or implemented.

- Plan contingencies in case your plans to change really fail. With a contingency plan you won't have to revert to the status quo for a restart.

- Show how changing will benefit others. This sometimes means spelling it out literally, "Here's what's in it for you!"

- Overcome self-defeating and related negative attitudes towards taking the risks that come with change.

- Develop the new communities in which to market ideas.

- Prepare for objection, and doubters.

- Develop plans for continuous improvement or innovation beyond the next change.

- Be flexible.

- Calculate the amount of risk in a proposed change.

- Consider a small change if a large one is too radical or risky.

The status quo can be a big enemy facing you every day. When the challenge of any change comes to mind, the comfort zone pops its head up, and encourages us to do the same things, the same way, resisting any change, and preventing any new opportunities or benefits to result.

Breaking through the status quo state can come as a result of many things. You can break through and gain inspiration from something in your youth. Thinking about something in the future can be a driving force behind a breakthrough. Sometimes a breakthrough happens because of something inside you — your values, beliefs, attitudes, or thoughts. Many, if not most, people want to change things for the better. Many, if not most, want more than the existing state of affairs.

Ten Breakthrough Strategies to Fight the Status Quo:

1. Do not complain or talk negatively about anything unless you also have a recommendation for a change to make things better.

2. Overcome the least attitude of, "That's the way I've always done it." No change means no break away from the current state of affairs.

3. Use the blank check or magic wand approach to removes all limits, inhibitions, excuses, or reasons why a change in the existing condition can't happen. You don't really have an unlimited supply of money or magical power; this technique supports brainstorming. Imaging how change, innovation, and breakthroughs can happen becomes easy.

4. There is no time like the present. Creating a sense of urgency will help you ask those all-important questions that challenge the current situation.

5. Consult with others to gain new and/or confirming perspectives in your thoughts that challenge the existing state of affairs.

6. Drill down for specifics and details. Continue to challenge with questions like, "So what?" and "What does that mean?" or "Why is that important?"

7. Repeat, rehearse, redo when necessary to clearly communicate a situation (use of Re words intended).

8. Give yourself and others permission to change. It's OK.

9. Taking baby steps is also OK. Lots of mini successes lead to larger breakthroughs.

10. Do it again. Challenging the status quo is a process not necessarily an event. Continual improvement comes from a continual challenge to the status quo.

In breakthrough strategy #2 above, the attitude of "tradition" or folklore was mentioned as it related to doing things the way they've always been done. The folklore attitude exists because the way things have always been done is easy. Not challenging the way things are in the current sense is certainly less controversial, but it will not move you forward. Controversy is good. Controversy can change things. To move in any direction, status quo must be challenged. To challenge something means taking initiative. We call these challenge initiatives.

Challenge Initiative Examples:

- Starting an association, fan club, or community
- Undertaking a brand new project unlike anything you've ever done before
- Continuing to ask the question, "So what?" until you drill down to the heart of an issue or opportunity
- Encouraging others to lead
- Removing yourself from situations for a period of time; stepping away to get a fresh perspective

Improve the Future by Disturbing the Present

Catherine Booth, co-founder of The Salvation Army, is a loud advocate of changing and disrupting the status quo. Catherine states, "There is no improving the future without disturbing the present."

While is it easy to stay in the "existing state of affairs" mode, nothing extraordinary in your personal or professional life can be done until you decide or take action to challenge the status quo. Nothing extraordinary can be done unless you disturb your present.

The National is the Abu Dhabi Media company's first English-language publication printed in Abu Dhabi, UAE. In February 2010, Journalist Chris Stanton reported in an article, "Success is Questioning Status Quo." Stanton led off his article by stating that we have all felt that twinge of wonder and disappointment —the "Why didn't I think of that?" moment —that comes with seeing a great business idea take off. He then reported on recent related research. "Dr Hal Gregersen, a professor at the Abu Dhabi branch of INSEAD, the French business school, set out to find what enables some people to turn promising ideas into profitable businesses. He and two colleagues have interviewed and studied executives known for their creativity, such as Steve Jobs of Apple and Jeff Bezos of Amazon. Dr. Gregersen now hopes to bring his findings to Abu Dhabi, where business opportunities and investment capital abound, but the individual drive for innovation is often stifled."

Stanton reported that Dr. Gregersen stated, "If we want Abu Dhabi to have a future 30 to 40 years from now, we have to build a capacity that doesn't exist today." Stanton went on to say that Dr. Gregersen and his colleagues surveyed 3,500 executives and creative individuals, and closely tracked the habits of 25 exceptional entrepreneurs to figure out the qualities that set the great innovators apart from the rest of the pack. In the article, Stanton said the researchers found that "this class of entrepreneurs is obsessed with questioning the status quo and suggesting radical changes, even when an existing product is generating healthy profits. They are often tinkerers and fearless about experimentation from a young age, and hold fast to their curiosity about new ideas in their professional life, whether at a cocktail party or a board meeting."

Entrepreneurs seem to stand out from typical managers in business. "Most managers actually don't want people to innovate," he reported Gregerson as saying. "A lot of managers give off this aura of 'just shut up'."

Dr. Gregersen's findings go on to report that for firms with a culture of innovation, the chief executive himself is the major source of new ideas, difficult questions and challenges for his employees. Executives good at managing day-to-day operations—the "MBAs," according to to Dr Gregersen - are balanced against individuals who bring fresh ideas into the office.

In the UAE and the wider region, Stanton reports that encouraging innovation and entrepreneurship is considered a key goal of government officials as they prepare to build a sustainable, post-oil economy. Stanton concludes that, "In the long run, innovation lies at the heart of a successful economy. The competitive advantage is the innovation process, the sustainable part is that capability can be passed on to others."

From Einstein to Star Trek

Doing something extraordinary related to innovation means going above and beyond, reaching new heights and taking your own problem-solving and creativity to a whole new level. Think Star Trek. Most remember the well-known quote from the series, "boldly going where no man has ever gone before." The full quotation was delivered as: "Space... the Final Frontier. These are the voyages of the starship *Enterprise*. It's five-year mission: to explore strange new worlds; to seek out new life, and new civilizations, to boldly go where no man has gone before." This certainly exemplified going above and beyond, reaching new heights of innovation and doing something extraordinary, beyond the existing state of affairs. Where can you go where no man has gone before?

When Albert Einstein told us to challenge authority, he really was saying challenge the status quo. Many people and many businesses have not reached new levels because they hold on to the routine; to the way things have always been done. For these people, the world passes them by, while they more or less just tread water.

Change takes a spark of creativity, a spirit of innovation, or just a frustration with the norm. Driven people and driven companies always want more —more than the current state of affairs. Wanting more results is challenging the status quo.

One breakthrough strategy that will challenge your current state of affairs is asking lots of questions, especially those questions that begin with, "What if…?" Encourage others, professionals and personal friends and family, to ask the "What if" question about anything and everything that might lead to change to current situations. Ask yourself, "Want a new current state of affairs? What if something changed? What if we did something different and not the way it's always been done before?"

↳ Learning the Status Quo

Author Unknown

Start with a cage containing five monkeys. In the cage, hang a banana on a string and put stairs under it. Before long, a monkey will go to the stairs and start to climb towards the banana. As soon as he touches the stairs, spray all of the monkeys with cold water...

After a while, another monkey will make an attempt with the same response - all of the monkeys are sprayed with cold water. Keep this up for several days.

Turn off the cold water. If, later, another monkey tries to climb the stairs, the other monkeys will try to prevent it even though no water sprays them.

Now, remove one monkey from the cage and replace it with a new one. The new monkey sees the banana and wants to climb the stairs. To his horror, all of the other monkeys attack him. After another attempt and attack, he knows that if he tries to climb the stairs, he will be assaulted.

Next, remove another of the original five monkeys and replace it with a new one. The newcomer goes to the stairs and is attacked. The previous newcomer takes part in the punishment with enthusiasm.

Replace the third original monkey with a new one. The new one makes it to the stairs and is attacked as well. Two of the four monkeys that beat him have no idea why they were not permitted to climb the stairs, or why they are participating in the beating of the newest monkey.

After replacing the fourth and fifth original monkeys, all the monkeys which have been sprayed with cold water have been replaced. Nevertheless, no monkey ever again approaches the stairs.

Why not?

"Because that's the way it's always been done around here."

About the Author

Al Lautenslager is best known as the best-selling co-author of *Guerrilla Marketing in 30 Days*. Al is also an award winning marketing/PR consultant, a much in-demand speaker and entrepreneur. He is the principal of a Market For Profits, an Appleton, Wisconsin based marketing consulting firm and a multiple, "Business of the Year" award winner as a business owner.

In addition to Al's articles appearing on numerous websites, he is a featured marketing and PR expert for the online version of *Entrepreneur Magazine* and a certified Guerrilla Marketing Coach.

Al is the author of *The Ultimate Guide to Direct Marketing* and numerous other marketing and business books. His latest venture is as CEO of CertifiedSocialMedia.com, a social media marketing educational and certification company. Al has worked with Donald Trump and *The Apprentice* and appears regularly on radio and TV including numerous media appearances every year, reviewing Super Bowl TV commercials.

His leadership has extended to his involvement on the board of directors of numerous non-profit organizations.

Other Books By
Al Lautenslager

Guerrilla Marketing In 30 Days

Guerrilla Marketing In 30 Days Workbook

Guerrilla Marketing In 30 Days – Audio CD

Guerrilla Marketing In 30 Days – Kindle E-book

Ultimate Guide to Direct Marketing

Kick It Up a Notch Marketing: 25 High Impact Marketing Strategies for Real Estate Professionals

SPECIAL OFFER To All RE: Readers

All readers of RE: The Book are entitled to a "special fee" presentation by Al Lautenslager, entitled, "Re-Invent This!" Ideal for conferences, keynotes, break-out sessions or seminars. Contact the author at the website address below.

All readers of RE: The Book are entitled to a free 1-hour Reinvention, Renewal, Repositioning consultation with the author. Contact Al through the website below.

Read more about Reinvention, Repositioning, Renewal and Rejuvenation. "Like" the Facebook Fan Page:

http://www.facebook.com/ReTheBook

Come Visit us at:

www.Re-The-Book.com

or

www.ReTheBookOnline.com

to claim your special offers today!

BUY A SHARE OF THE FUTURE IN YOUR COMMUNITY

These certificates make great holiday, graduation and birthday gifts that can be personalized with the recipient's name. The cost of one S.H.A.R.E. or one square foot is $54.17. The personalized certificate is suitable for framing and will state the number of shares purchased and the amount of each share, as well as the recipient's name. The home that you participate in "building" will last for many years and will continue to grow in value.

Here is a sample SHARE certificate:

HABITAT FOR HUMANITY

THIS CERTIFIES THAT

YOUR NAME HERE

HAS INVESTED IN A HOME FOR A DESERVING FAMILY

1985-2010

TWENTY-FIVE YEARS OF BUILDING FUTURES
IN OUR COMMUNITY ONE HOME AT A TIME

1200 SQUARE FOOT HOUSE @ $65,000 = $54.17 PER SQUARE FOOT
This certificate represents a tax-deductible donation. It has no cash value.

YES, I WOULD LIKE TO HELP!

I support the work that Habitat for Humanity does and I want to be part of the excitement! As a donor, I will receive periodic updates on your construction activities but, more importantly, I know my gift will help a family in our community realize the dream of homeownership. **I would like to SHARE in your efforts against substandard housing in my community!** *(Please print below)*

PLEASE SEND ME _____ SHARES at $54.17 EACH = $ $_____

In Honor Of: _____

Occasion: (Circle One)   HOLIDAY   BIRTHDAY   ANNIVERSARY

     OTHER: _____

Address of Recipient: _____

Gift From: _____ *Donor Address:* _____

Donor Email: _____

I AM ENCLOSING A CHECK FOR $ $_____ **PAYABLE TO HABITAT FOR HUMANITY OR PLEASE CHARGE MY VISA OR MASTERCARD** *(CIRCLE ONE)*

Card Number _____ Expiration Date: _____

Name as it appears on Credit Card _____ Charge Amount $ _____

Signature _____

Billing Address _____

Telephone # Day _____ Eve _____

PLEASE NOTE: Your contribution is tax-deductible to the fullest extent allowed by law.
Habitat for Humanity • P.O. Box 1443 • Newport News, VA 23601 • 757-596-5553
www.HelpHabitatforHumanity.org

Printed in the USA
CPSIA information can be obtained
at www.ICGtesting.com
JSHW082214140824
68134JS00014B/611

9 781600 379925